Foreword

It gives me great pleasure to write a forward to *Willing and Able*. This resource for teachers and community leaders recognises and encapsulates the spirit of the Disability Discrimination Act: the promotion and protection of the right of people who have disabilities to equal opportunity for involvement in all aspects of living in our society.

People who have disabilities are, first and foremost, people. They have precisely the same concerns, enjoyments, aspirations and struggles with life that are shared by all their peers. As one who used to be brought in and out of the rain, apparently in the belief that I may shrink, and who was protected against the ordinary bumps, risks and disappointments of life, I am very pleased to see teachers and community leaders encouraged to experiment and discover imaginative ways to create sport and recreational environments in which all people are equally enabled to participate and contribute, tumble and strive, succeed and fail.

On reading through *Willing and able* I was delighted to see such statements as 'they too have the right to acquire bumps and bruises', acknowledgment that all people benefit from sport and physical activity as an ordinary part of life, and an emphasis on the equal right to choose how to spend one's time. There are also some perceptive and funny contributions from those who are old enough to reflect on their own childhood and to offer some guidance to modern service providers.

Comments from teachers, coaches and community leaders indicate that they benefit professionally from the challenge to their theory and practice so that they become better providers all round, more able to meet the various needs of their infinitely various populations, with and without disabilities.

All these things make *Willing and Able* an accessible and interesting resource. It is more than that, however: it answers questions about a range of disabilities, gives information about areas where special care must be taken, and abounds with hints and ideas to be put into practice.

People who have disabilities are often delivered 'sports services' as though sport were yet another form of therapy. This takes the enjoyment out of the activity, and denies participants the ordinary 'personal best' and other competitive challenges which most people take for granted in playing sport. *Willing and Able* recognises that people who have disabilities play sport for the same reasons as everybody: to have fun, to use up the abundant energy of youth, to get fit, and, if possible, to win. In promoting this recognition and in helping people who may be involved in the world of sport to create truly inclusive sporting and recreational environments for everyone, this manual is, indeed, a winner.

Elizabeth Hastings
Former Disability Discrimination Commissioner

After a battle against cancer Elizabeth Hastings died in November 1998, aged 54. Permission to retain this forward, written in 1995, for the second edition of this manual was provided by her family in her memory.

Contents

Foreword iii

Preface ix

Acknowledgments x

Introduction 1

   Introducing Willing and Able 3

   Why Willing and Able? 4

   Disability Education Program and Active Australia 5

   Program resources 6

   Willing and Able training 8

Section 1: Getting started 9

   1.1   Do sport and physical activity disadvantage people with disabilities? ... 14

   1.2   Disabilities — some facts 15

   1.3   Disadvantage — what can we do about it? 17

   1.4   Inclusion and integration — is there a difference? 18

   1.5   Why include? 19

   1.6   Physical activity for all — the inclusion process 20

   1.7   Terminology 23

Section 2: Getting ready for school 25

   2.1   Adapting and modifying physical activity at school 28

      2.1.1   Active Australia Schools Network 28

      2.1.2   Inclusion in the school environment 28

      2.1.3   The Golden Rule of Inclusion 30

      2.1.4   How do I go about planning for individual needs? 32

      2.1.5   Developing a planning model 42

      2.1.6   Abilities-based assessment 47

   2.2   Running inclusive activities 49

      2.2.1   Early childhood to lower primary 49

      2.2.2   Primary 56

      2.2.3   Secondary to post-compulsory 64

      2.2.4   Young people with high support needs 69

      2.2.5   Young people with degenerative conditions 74

Section 3: Opening doors for people with disabilities.......75

3.1 Introduction..79
    3.1.1 Links between schools and clubs...........................80
    3.1.2 Establishing closer relationships with schools.........80
3.2 What's behind the door?...83
    3.2.1 Why include people with disabilities?...................83
    3.2.2 What's in it for me — the individual....................83
    3.2.3 What's in it for me — the organisation................83
    3.2.4 Other things to consider..................................87
3.3 Is your door open?...90
    3.3.1 What is accessibility?.....................................90
    3.3.2 The audit..93
3.4 Locksmith's report..94
    3.4.1 Developing an audit.......................................94
    3.4.2 Attitudes of club members...............................96
    3.4.3 Orientation...97
    3.4.4 Fitting in..97
    3.4.5 Physical accessibility.....................................98
3.5 Impressive doorknobs, shiny keys...............................100
    3.5.1 Target groups...100
    3.5.2 Develop your product....................................101
    3.5.3 Reach out..101

Section 4: Implications for sport and physical activity.......105

4.1 Amputations...107
4.2 Asthma...108
4.3 Attention deficit hyperactivity disorder........................111
4.4 Autism...114
4.5 Cancer...116
4.6 Cerebral palsy...119
4.7 Cystic fibrosis..122
4.8 Deafness and being hard of hearing.............................123
4.9 Diabetes...126
4.10 Down syndrome...129
4.11 Emotional disturbances..131
4.12 Epilepsy..133
4.13 HIV/AIDS and blood disorders...................................136
4.14 Juvenile rheumatoid arthritis and osteoporosis................137
4.15 Mental health..139
4.16 Muscular dystrophy..142
4.17 Obesity...144
4.18 Schizophrenia..145

4.19 Spina bifida..148

4.20 Spinal cord injuries...151

4.21 Transplants...153

4.22 Vision impairment...154

References and further resources

References and further resources................................159

Contacts/help

Contacts/help..161

Appendices

1   Disability Education Program state coordinator contact list.............163

2   Lifting techniques...164

3   Schools Network membership form....................................166

4   School environment/ethos form.......................................167

5   Independence graph..168

6   School community links form...169

7   Curriculum teaching and learning policy form.....................170

8   Client focus checklist...171

9   Human resources checklist..172

10 Audit sheet..173

11 Quality of service checklist...175

List of tables

1   School environment/ethos..32

2   General activity adaptations...34

3   School community links...41

4   Planning for inclusion...43

5   Curriculum teaching and learning......................................45

6   Abilities-based assessment form.......................................48

7   Sample client focus checklist..85

8   Sample human resource checklist......................................91

9   Sample audit sheet..95

10 Sample quality of service checklist....................................99

11 Dealing with an acute asthma attack................................110

12 Degrees of hearing loss...123

List of figures

1   The inclusion process..21

2   Review and modification..21

3   Positioning of the shunt..149

4   Functional activities related to spinal cord segments C1–S4.....151

Preface

Give it a Go is the revised edition of the *Willing and Able* manual, *An Introduction to Inclusive Practices*. *An Introduction to Inclusive Practices* was published in 1995 and focused on school-based strategies to help teachers include young people with disabilities in regular physical activity programs. Since that time Willing and Able has evolved dramatically to encompass a much broader range of issues and settings. A national program has been created providing opportunities for all providers in sport and physical activity to gain access to training and education. Further resources have been produced to cover specific issues, including CD ROM and online versions of the training modules. Willing and Able has joined forces with the *Coaching Athletes with Disabilities* scheme to form the Disability Education Program under the framework of Active Australia.

To reflect this evolution *Give it a Go* attempts to advance our thinking and practice on issues of inclusion and covers a wider range of settings, from school-based to sport and recreation clubs and organisations. It covers all ages and expands on previous material — for example, cancer and mental health issues have been added to section four. The original format and style of the manual have been retained; the user friendly approach has proved successful in the past.

Give it a Go can be used as a stand alone resource or a text to accompany the training package. Either way, the manual attempts to provide readers with added confidence, knowledge and skills so that they can give the inclusion of people with a disability a real go.

Peter Downs
Manager, Disability Education
Australian Sports Commission

Acknowledgments

The Australian Sports Commission expresses its appreciation to the authors
Peter Downs, Kelli Chilton, Susie Bennett-Yeo, Dale Lanini, Kathy Tessier, Robyn Floyd
and Peter Stewart for compiling the required information and writing this manual.

Thanks are also extended to the teachers, students, administrators and volunteers who
have contributed to the *Willing and Able* project.

In addition, we gratefully acknowledge the contribution of:

Paul Walthers, Claire Whitwer-Smith, Eric Russell, Nicholas Bailey, Debbie Toman,
Lara Hayes, Ryan Sherry, Darryl Little, Richard Lockwood, Cathy White,
Darren Cunningham, Leah Page, Anthony Nichols, Hamish Macdonald,
Dusty Macgraw, Lyn Phillips and other Sport Development staff of the
Australian Sports Commission who have helped along the way.

Introduction

Contents

1 Introducing Willing and Able   3

2 Why Willing and Able?   4

3 Disability Education Program and Active Australia   5

4 Program resources   6

5 Willing and Able training   8

'A difference is a difference only when it makes a difference'

1 Introducing Willing and Able

Getting involved in sport and physical activity is something many thousands of Australians do every year. It is a part of our culture and way of life. This is no different for people with disabilities. More and more people with disabilities are getting involved and getting active. This is good for people with disabilities, good for sport and good for the community generally. As more people with disabilities get active, sport and physical activity providers are finding out something that many people with disabilities have known for some time. Sport and physical activity providers often need support in finding ways to appropriately include people with disabilities in their programs and services.

Willing and Able is a project of the Australian Sports Commission's Disability Education Program. It is a project set up to help teachers and community leaders to include people with disabilities in sport and physical activity in the most appropriate manner possible.

The Disability Education Program is a tool of Active Australia, the national initiative designed to encourage more Australians to become physically active. The other tool of the Disability Education Program is the Coaching Athletes with Disabilities (CAD) Scheme. These programs are delivered across the country in a series of short courses available for anyone involved or interested in the inclusion of people with disabilities in sport and physical activity programs.

AUSTRALIAN
SPORTS
COMMISSION

ACTIVE
AUSTRALIA

Disability Education Program

Willing and Able

Coaching Athletes
with a Disability

2   Why 'Willing and Able'?

Simply because more and more people with disabilities will be taking part in regular sport and physical activity programs.

The need to provide assistance with planning and conducting sport and physical activity programs that include people with a disability has been a prominent and often repeated message from providers across Australia. This call for support has intensified in recent years as the trend toward deinstitutionalisation and mainstreaming has increased.

A legal obligation

The Australian Sports Commission also recognises that there is now a legal obligation on teachers and community leaders to provide the same opportunity for all people. Under the 1992 *Disability Discrimination Act* (DDA)[1], people with disabilities have the right to take part in sporting activities in the same way as people without disabilities.

This means that people with disabilities cannot be excluded from playing sport (taking part in activities) if they are:

- capable of playing the sport (taking part in the activity), or

- selected to play the sport on the basis of their skills and abilities.

For example:

> *If a young person has the necessary skills to play cricket or to swim competitively, they cannot be excluded because they have asthma or are deaf.*

Basically, the DDA focuses on the effect of the disability rather than the cause.

Furthermore, the DDA requires educators to offer the same opportunities in education (including physical education) for all persons. Judgements should not be made on what it is perceived the young person cannot do. Significantly, the DDA also protects people against discrimination which denies or limits access on the grounds of the disability.

For example:

> *Not allowing a young person in a wheelchair to take part in a basketball lesson simply because access to the gymnasium is via a flight of stairs.*

---

1   Further information on the DDA is contained in the booklet *Harassment-free sport: anti-disability discrimination* (1999), which is available from the Australian Sports Commission, tel (02) 6214 1915, email pubs@ausport.gov.au

3   Disability Education Program and Active Australia

Active Australia is a national initiative designed to encourage more Australians to become physically active. Its basis is a shared approach by a range of organisations aimed at getting Australians involved in quality physical activity. Active Australia focuses on two main areas — encouraging people to be more physically active, and working to improve the places where people can be active. The principles of access and equity underpin Active Australia and are paramount to its core philosophy. Willing and Able, through its resources and training packages, works in both areas through collaboration and practical hands-on delivery. The concept of inclusion stretches across all physical activity environments and into all settings.

The core philosophy of the Disability Education Program is one that concerns a range of interrelated issues, including access, equity, participation, choice, opportunity, human rights, dignity and empowerment.

The most common perspective that has shaped common sense and legal under-standings of disability has been the medical model. This perspective emphasises an individual's inabilities to adapt to an essentially normal environment. Disability in this sense is a personal tragedy that results in images of helplessness and inferiority.

> 'We are seen as "abnormal" because we are different; we are problem people, lacking the equipment for social integration. But the truth is, like everybody else, we have a range of things we can and cannot do, a range of abilities both mental and physical that are unique to us as individuals. The only difference between us and other people is that we are viewed through spectacles that only focus on our inabilities, and which suffer an automatic blindness — a sort of social reflex — regarding our abilities.'
>
> Brissenden (1986) 175

The main problem of this kind of perspective is that people with disabilities are compared to a perceived notion of normality. The implication is that, by not being normal, people with disabilities need to change in order to catch up with the able-bodied world. It is also, clearly, a false perspective in that no account is made of the sociopolitical aspects of disability. The medical model is a model born out of a predominantly able-bodied society.

> 'All disabled people experience disability as social restriction, whether those restrictions occur as a consequence of inaccessible built environments, questionable notions of intelligence and social competence, the inability of the general public to use sign language, the lack of reading material in braille or hostile public attitudes to people with non-visible disabilities.'
>
> Oliver (1990) 15

The Disability Education Program encapsulates a social/human rights model of disability. Here, the perceived problems of disability emanate, not from individual pathology, but from social restriction and a handicapping environment. The approach of the Disability Education Program is one that largely addresses environmental handicap as it relates to sport and physical activity. As such, it addresses directly the places where people can be active and helps generic service providers to cater for a greater diversity of customer than ever before.

The Willing and Able project is intended for anyone interested or involved in the provision of sporting opportunities and/or physical activities that include people with disabilities. The project resources and training packages are of use to teachers, coaches, sports organisations, community groups, local government agencies and students.

We have made the resources as practical as possible. This book, *Give it a Go*, is the core resource for the project. Willing and Able aims to:

> *provide a national network of education and support for sport and physical activity providers to increase their confidence, knowledge and skills, to create better opportunities for more people with disabilities.*

More specifically, *Give it a Go* provides information for schools, organisations and individuals to assist them in making sport and physical activity an accessible and enjoyable thing to do for people with disabilities.

4 Program resources

This manual can be used by itself, or as the main text for short courses that operate nationally.

Other Willing and Able resources include:

Getting Ready Kit — a disability awareness kit designed to prepare service providers with the tools to appropriately include people with disabilities into regular physical activity programs. The kit consists of 17 information cards. Of these, 13 are student and teacher learning cards and four are specifically for teacher reference.

Getting Ready Kit (1997)
A3 sheets in folder, col,
ISBN 0 642 25887 2,
$19.50

Teachers Talk About:... experiences of inclusive physical activity. Deals with the real life day-to-day experiences of teachers who provide sport and physical activity programs for children. The teachers' stories in this book offer solutions, useful information and a critical understanding of inclusive practice and the needs of individuals with a disability.

Teachers Talk About... (1998): 60pp, b/w ISBN 0 642 25887, **$116**

Count Me In CD ROM is designed for pre-service and practicing teachers and others with an interest in providing quality programs for all children, including those with a disability. A series of case studies explores attitudes to disability and inclusion, outlines the hallmarks of inclusive practice and explains the principles of successful inclusion.

Count Me In CD ROM ISBN 0 86422 682 1, **$43**

Opening Doors: Getting people with a disability involved in sport and recreation This book aims to provide sport and recreation organisations with some practical information and ideas about including people with a disability in sport and recreation. A series of case studies explores the strategies employed by generic service providers to attract and retain people with disabilities as members.

Opening Doors (2000) 76pp, ISBN 1 74013 019 7, **$16**

5 Willing and Able training

The training courses that operate around the country are an important part of the Willing and Able program. All Disability Education Program courses are divided into modules that follow a similar format and are designed to last three hours.

Module 1   *Count Me In*

A general sport, physical activity and disability awareness workshop suitable for anyone wanting to include people with disabilities in regular sport and physical activity programs.

Module 2   *Getting Ready for School*

A practical physical education and sport awareness workshop examining the issues of inclusion from early childhood to post-compulsory years of schooling. The module is suitable for teachers.

Module 3   *Opening Doors for People with Disabilities*

A workshop suitable for sport and recreation club officials, administrators and volunteers who examine strategies to attract and retain people with disabilities as members.

An experienced network of coordinators in each state (see Contacts) manages and delivers courses. The coordinators can work with you to adapt courses to suit your group's needs.

An online version of Module 1 is available on http://cls.tmpwlearning.com. Contact the National Coordinator, tel. (02) 6214 1792 or email dep@ausport.gov.au

Section 1
Getting Started

Contents

1.1 Do sport and physical activity disadvantage people with disabilities?   **14**

1.2 Disabilities — some facts   **15**

1.3 Disadvantage — what can we do about it?   **17**

1.4 Inclusion and integration — is there a difference?   **18**

1.5 Why include?   **19**

1.6 Physical activity for all — the inclusion process   **20**

1.7 Terminology   **23**

'If we accept the premise that all people are special, we are better able to deal with individual differences in different individuals'

Kevin Coombs

I became a paraplegic when I was 13 in 1954, after a shooting accident in country New South Wales.

I was sent to the Royal Children's Hospital in Melbourne for a time, and then transferred to the Austin Hospital when the Spinal Unit was started there under the director Dr David Cheshire.

Dr Cheshire had studied under Sir Ludwig Guttman who established a world-famous spinal injuries centre at Stoke Mandeville in England, and continued those philosophies at the Austin Hospital.

As well as gym work we participated in a wide range of sports — swimming, weightlifting, baseball, field events, archery, and basketball which was my main sport.

I was selected for the Australian Wheelchair basketball team to compete at the first Paralympics in Rome in 1960. During my sporting career I competed in five Paralympics and numerous other international competitions.

I retired from international competition in 1988.

On a national level I played in every Victorian team from 1960 until I retired from national competition in 1990.

I was captain of the Australian team on several occasions and have been national Best and Fairest twice.

In 1984 I was awarded an OAM for my services to disabled sport and Aboriginal services.

In 1964 Paravics sport club, now known as Wheelchair Sports Victoria, was formed. I was a foundation member and then served on the board of directors.

In 1998 I was honoured to have 'Kevin Coombs Avenue' at the Olympic complex in Sydney named after me.

It gives me a great deal of satisfaction to think I have helped with the development of wheelchair sport in Australia to the level we have today.

Participating in sport gave me many advantages that still evident today. I have many friends Australia-wide I have known for 40 years, I have had travel and experiences worldwide, I enjoy good health and I have had a very satisfying and productive professional life.

I have recently retired from full-time work and look forward to new challenges.

Getting started

Meet Stephen, Jane, Nicholas, Fran, Joanne, Rahul and Dave. Like all young people they have unique abilities and needs. These young people are the stars of *Give it a Go*.

They will feature throughout the book. We will grow up with them; we will plan for their inclusion into sport and physical activity programs; we will look at running various activity sessions with them from early childhood to post-compulsory years of schooling. We will look at how sport and recreation organisations go about providing for their needs and we will consider the specific implications relating to their conditions, for their inclusion into regular physical activity sessions.

Stephen *is a lively young man who enjoys expressing himself through movement. Stephen mostly looks after himself for the activities of daily living and has figured out a way of doing things, like tying shoe laces, even though his right arm and wrist are permanently bent and he has little manual dexterity in his fingers. He is very popular with his school mates as he likes to play jokes and always tries his hardest in activities. Stephen's lower right leg is also permanently bent outwards with his foot twisted inward, making balancing a problem. His speech is slurred and his vision impaired. Stephen has cerebral palsy but has always attended regular schools.*

Even though **Jane** *tires quite easily she is prepared to have a go at most activities. Her main sports are basketball and softball as she has very good eye-hand coordination. Although she has to use a wheelchair for getting around most of the time, she does use leg braces and crutches. Her upper body strength is good but she has very little sensation in her lower body. Jane takes part in most activities in regular school although she still takes time off for physical therapy. Jane requires regular catheterisation for toileting. She is quiet and very conscious of her difference, particularly during PE lessons. At birth Jane had a tube inserted between the brain and the stomach to drain the regular build-up of excess fluid. She also has vision and perception problems as she is slightly cross-eyed. Jane was born with spina bifida.*

Although **Nicholas** *has been legally blind since birth he does have light perception and can make out shapes at a distance. He is keen on all forms of physical activity, particularly running. He performs well in most areas of school life and can read braille. It is quite normal for Nicholas to have cuts and bruises on elbows and knees and he shrugs off with a smile daily knocks and bashes.*

Fran's teachers have great difficulty gaining her attention, particularly during lengthy explanations and demonstrations. She seems confused easily and appears to be daydreaming a lot of the time. It is difficult to know if she is enjoying activities or not as most of the time she is very expressionless and quiet. Fran also seems to forget where to be and what to do even if the activity has been performed before. Fran has been in and out of special and regular schools, though her parents prefer that she be fully included into her local school. Fran is autistic.

Dave lives in a rural area with few facilities for sport and physical activity. He obviously enjoys sport most of the time although he becomes frustrated by his poor coordination and balance during certain activities. His teachers also get frustrated, mostly by his mood swings and lethargy. He is often away sick, complaining of headaches and fatigue, and is not always comfortable in large groups where he becomes shy and introverted. Dave's diabetes is largely controlled through medication although his teachers need to be constantly aware of his health status, particularly before exercise and given his quietness and lethargy regarding his diet. Dave also has a conductive hearing loss that makes following some speech difficult.

When she was very young **Joanne** was involved in a car accident that left her paralysed down the left side of her body. She really enjoys playing with her friends and hates to be left out. She uses her wheelchair most of the time and needs assistance on tricky or uneven surfaces. She has slurred speech which sometimes makes it difficult to understand what she is saying if you are not used to her, and has difficulty under-standing and following directions. Joanne shows great determination, however, in everything she does and will not give up easily.

Rahul is a cheerful young man who enjoys all forms of activity. His general fitness level, however, is not good and he tires quite easily. Rahul is generally very affectionate with everyone he meets and can get upset if people are not so friendly to him. His academic achievements are not good as he has difficulty understanding basic concepts. This is not helped by his hearing and vision impairments. He also has a condition called atlantoaxial instability, that is commonly associated with Down syndrome, which means the cervical vertebrae are not aligned properly. This precludes him from certain activities and causes him some discomfort, especially in winter.

This section briefly considers some general concepts and terms related to people with disabilities. It is often the case that literature relating to disability issues is complicated by unnecessary jargon. Here, terms and explanations will be kept deliberately brief and where possible practical examples will be given to illustrate points.

We will consider how people with disabilities are disadvantaged in sport and physical activity — specifically, where disadvantage comes from and what influences it. To help understand this we will look at a model of integration and inclusion.

> *'I'm somewhat surprised about how far I've come in short period. It's hard to imagine why I was so afraid and uneasy at the beginning. I realise that one day as a teacher I will be confronted with children with disabilities and vow to myself that I will be understanding and do my best to adapt my lessons for them. This experience has opened my eyes to the fact that as teachers it is our responsibility to provide the best education for each individual ... I want to help make a difference.'*
>
> Patrick S, in Connolly (1994) 320

1.1 Do sport and physical activity disadvantage people with disabilities?

It is important to understand why people with disabilities experience disadvantage in sport and physical activity. It is important because without understanding the nature of disadvantage we are unable to do anything to minimise the disadvantage people with disabilities face. Ultimately this will help us to work with the things that people with disabilities can do. This is in contrast to the more traditional model of considering what people with disabilities cannot do or what it is perceived they cannot do.

So why are people with disabilities disadvantaged when it comes to sport and physical activity? History has shown that in virtually all aspects of society people with disabilities are disadvantaged. They do not enjoy the same level of opportunity as people without disabilities. The area of sport and physical activity is no exception to this. Various models and theories have been developed over the years to explain this.

Wolfensberger (1972) provided a useful overview of three theories of disability that have contributed to disadvantage.

- **Destruction**

  This view held that people with disabilities would experience life that 'was not worth living'. Somehow people with disabilities were categorised as evil and deviant and as such society needed to be protected from them. Society wanted to do away with disability altogether.

- **Segregation**

  The charity model of disability that emanated from the nineteenth century was based on an assumption that society should pity people with disabilities and that people with disabilities needed to be looked after and provided with special services. Segregated settings arose as a means of provision for people with disabilities.

- **Reversal or cure and prevention**

  The reversal or cure and prevention model is the basis of the medical approach to disability that still dominates today. Here, the problems of disability arise predominantly from individual pathology. The means to reduce the problem lies with curing or reducing the disability or the sick individual.

These models still have an impact today and contribute significantly to social and economic policy and, importantly, the underlying attitudes that disadvantage people with disabilities.

The social/human rights model basically asserts the rights of all individuals to equal opportunities, regardless of disability. The disadvantages that people with disabilities face are predominantly the result of an unaccepting and hostile environment. Environments and social norms are constructed on 'able-bodied' terms, thus excluding those who do not fit.

The benefit of this model is that the perceived problems of disability can be influenced by educating and adapting the environment so that people with disabilities do fit and do have equal opportunity where possible. **We can actually look outside the individual and their disability to the social and physical aspects that disadvantage people who have a disability.** With this mind set we are now in a position to do something about disadvantage.

1.2   Disabilities — some facts

Disabilities are either **congenital** or **acquired**. They occur before or during birth if they are congenital (Jane has a congenital disability) and after birth if they are acquired (Joanne has an acquired disability). A compressed umbilical cord during birth causing brain damage is an example of a congenital disability. Acquired disabilities usually occur as a result of illness or injury. The onset of periodic seizures as a result of head injury is an example of an acquired disability.

Disabilities do not necessarily last forever. They can be **acute** — a temporary condition from which a complete recovery is possible, such as a broken leg — or **chronic**, which means the condition is long term but not necessarily permanent, such as juvenile rheumatoid arthritis. Disabilities may also be permanent, such as Rahul's condition of Down syndrome or Fran's autism.

> '*V exhibits characteristics from a multitude of disorders. It is evident that categorisation may benefit the individual as treatment ... however it may be suggested that a classification of V's condition might deprive her of what she needs — to be treated as an individual, a child who is innocent and carefree, existing to play and grow, mentally and physically.*'
>
> Michelle B in Connolly (1994) 321

Some disabilities are **progressive** while others are **non-progressive**. Stephen has a non-progressive permanent disability, that is, the condition does not increase in extent or severity but is lifelong. Other disabilities do increase in extent and severity as time goes by and may even result in death.

The terms **mild, moderate** and **severe** are often used with reference to disability. They have been widely misused and misinterpreted as they were originally developed to help educationalists, welfare workers and medical practitioners keep records and undertake assessments.

Assessing the ability of each individual is far more important than any preoccupation with categories such as 'mild', 'moderate' and 'severe'.

Labelling or categorising can lead to situations where physical activity programs are designed in accord with inaccurate preconceived expectations of what an individual can do, rather than what they actually can do.

It is more relevant for teachers and community leaders to discuss the severity of the condition in relation to **support needs**, than to focus on the technical descriptions of 'mild', 'moderate' and 'severe'.

For example:

> Although **Fran** may be labelled as having a 'mild' intellectual disability she does have 'high' support needs (ie in terms of behaviour management). The label of 'mild', therefore, is misleading in terms working with Fran in activities.

While there are circumstances where labelling is necessary (eg for funding purposes) there are a number of disadvantages to labelling that you should be aware of. These include:

• labels emphasise what the young person cannot do rather than can do

• labels tend to make the problem permanent

• problems are associated with the individual rather than with the teaching method or the environment

• we have a tendency to overgeneralise characteristics associated with the disability (eg Dave has a short attention span, therefore all children with similar conditions have short attention spans)

• programs are designed for the label or category and not the individual

• labels encourage the setting of inappropriate expectations (ie underachievement)

• if placed in a group in accord with a label (eg mild, moderate or severe), young people may have lower functioning role models

1.3 Disadvantage — what can we do about it?

We have already considered the notion of disability and disadvantage. But how can we recognise where disadvantage occurs and what can we do about it? Disability may, or may not, lead to disadvantage:

> **Nicholas** *is legally blind (the disability), so he has difficulty following visual instruction (the disadvantage) and as a result has limited access to physical activity opportunities.*

Here, Nicholas's disadvantages are imposed on him because physical activity training is, in part, provided through visual instruction. However, if alternative teaching strategies were employed where emphasis is placed on spoken feedback and manual demonstration, there would be no meaningful disadvantage. **The disadvantage was the result of poor teaching strategies.**

Let's look at another example.

> **Stephen** *wants to play in the school volleyball team and has little movement in his right arm (the disability). He has practised and is proficient in using his left arm only for spiking, setting etc (no disadvantage in this context). He is still perceived as being unable to play in the volleyball team.*

Stephen's disability does not affect his ability to perform the task. There is disadvantage, however, imposed by the school's attitude toward the disability. It is possible that this action could be viewed as discrimination under the 1992 *Disability Discrimination Act*.

It is useful to consider the following:

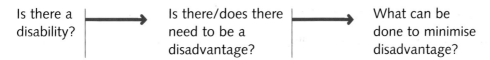

Is there a disability? ⟶ Is there/does there need to be a disadvantage? ⟶ What can be done to minimise disadvantage?

This will help you consider if there is any disadvantage present. It should also help you start to consider solutions.

1.4 Inclusion and integration — is there a difference?

The term **inclusion** is relatively new to Australia. The terms **integration** and **mainstreaming** have been used more frequently and describe the processes by which people with disabilities are placed in regular physical activity programs. While Willing and Able firmly adopts a philosophy of inclusion, it recognises that other terms are often used to describe very much the same thing. Inclusion should also be viewed as a temporary concept. The notion that programs are permanently inclusive suggests that young people with disabilities are being accommodated and that changes to the regular program are necessary. An inclusive program should be **the** regular program that does not need constant change to accommodate certain individuals.

For the purposes of Willing and Able, however, inclusion, integration and mainstreaming are understood in the following ways:

- **Inclusion**

  To 'include' is defined in the Oxford English dictionary as 'to comprise or embrace, as part of a whole'. Inclusive programs mean all people are provided with the opportunity to participate in sport and physical activity at the **appropriate level** and with the **appropriate** support. All people are part of the community and as such are embraced as part of a total system. Inclusion also means that people with disabilities are recognised as individuals with the right to take risks, to make choices, to make mistakes, to be independent and to reap the benefits of physical activity in the same way as any other person in the community.

- **Integration**

  According to the Oxford English Dictionary to integrate means to 'be made up of parts'. Integrated programming refers to the **placement** of people with disabilities in regular settings. The problem of integration understood in this way is that proximity itself cannot guarantee acceptance. People may be *integrated* but not necessarily *included*!

  In some early integrated programs young people were placed in regular settings because such placement required very little or no change to regular activities. The term 'dumping' was an expression coined by physical educators faced with inappropriately integrated students.

'At school you either joined in sports or you got five hundred lines and basically I didn't want to get left out. Even when the whole school was doing cross-country I had to go as well and do exactly the same course as the rest of them.'

David Swift: in Humphries and Gordon (1992) 54

- **Mainstreaming**

  Mainstreaming describes the **process** of integrating young people with disabilities into regular physical activity sessions. The process can be with or without appropriate support.

  'Inclusive physical education is a place where individual differences are not hidden or ridiculed but rather shared among students who learn to respect each other's limitations and unique abilities.'

  Block (1994) 16

Inclusion does not mean that young people with disabilities are placed in settings that are inappropriate to their individual needs. Inclusion means recognising individual differences and providing for those differences by adapting programs when necessary. These adaptations should be viewed as temporary.

1.5   Why include?

- Because the needs of all people are different. A person with a disability requires individualised instruction in the same way that all people require individualised instruction. Teachers, instructors and physical educators run activity sessions that cater for the needs of people with varying degrees of motor and intellectual function, regardless of disability. A person with a disability is just another member of the group.

  'We were all mad keen on playing football too ... Well when we played at school they used to pick two teams and nobody wanted me on their team. They used to stand arguing who was going to have me on their team. I would always be the one left over, feeling so embarrassed.'

  David Swift: in Humphries and Gordon (1992) 54

- Because segregated settings often duplicate resources. In many instances the needs of people with disabilities are the same as those of people without disabilities. While a system of segregated-inclusive-regular settings is necessary to support the wide spectrum of needs, a system that provides for all people in the one, most appropriate, setting is more efficient and cost-effective and fosters better social opportunities for all children.

- Because segregation can encourage stigmatisation. 'Special' segregated settings emphasise the physical, intellectual or sensory difference that separates some people from others. There are similarities and differences between all people. The disability is only one aspect of the person's character.

- Because people with disabilities benefit from a balanced program in the same ways as do all people. They benefit through improved fitness and health, through learning new skills, through increased social contacts and improved self-confidence and self-esteem.

- Because people who do not have a disability can learn about disabilities and appreciate individual differences better.

- Because people will learn that participating in activities in different ways does not lessen their value.

- Because all concerned will benefit, since inclusion recognises the value of the individual and provides all people with the 'dignity of risk', the ability to make choices and the opportunity to win or lose.

> *'I felt different. The others would sort of look at me. It was as if they saw me as inferior. That was how they made me feel. I wanted to join in but of course I couldn't. I tried very hard to keep up with the games but quite often I would end up sitting them out'*
>
> Christine Hollis: in Humphries and Gordon (1992) 38

1.6 Physical activity for all — the inclusion process

A major goal of any physical activity program should be to provide opportunities for all people to participate in the most appropriate manner possible. There are many factors that can determine the appropriateness of any given activity or program. The adjustments or modifications required to help existing activities or programs become appropriate are critical. This fine tuning can be small or large. You might do this on the spot by yourself or it might require extensive planning with a range of people.

Remember, it is important to view all modifications as temporary, as just another step toward a program that is suitable for all.

This does not mean that a certain modification will stop. It means it will become accepted as part of the regular program. The *Inclusion Process* below depicts a continual exercise of activity or program review and modification where the ultimate goal is to finish with an activity or program that is inclusive, but not actually labelled as such. It is a good quality activity or program that is suitable for all.

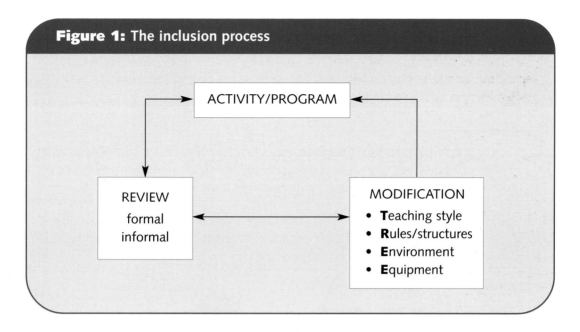

Figure 1: The inclusion process

Within the *Inclusion Process* there are various entry and exit points. For example, a review may mean an 'on the spot' modification made to a specific activity as the result of a judgement made by a teacher or coach. Or, it may mean a planned program change as the result of extensive consultation with a range of individuals. Either way, the inclusion process remains the same in that the regular activity or program is reviewed, a modification made and the new activity becomes the improved regular one. The process is a cyclical and continuous one in this way.

Here, we will examine the *Inclusion Process* in more detail.

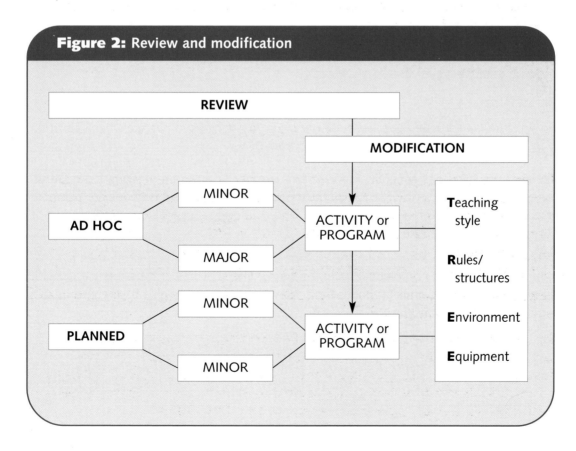

Figure 2: Review and modification

Reviews can be made in a variety of ways. They are not necessarily planned. They may be a thought process at a particular time. A review can be made by an individual, as the activity is happening, or by a small group of key people responsible for an individualised program. The reviews can be minor or major and can affect an activity or a program.

For example:

> During a throwing activity **Stephen** experiences difficulties with balance and repeatedly falls over. Two coaches quickly decide that some support is needed and use a chair to provide balance on the right side.

Modifications can be very diverse. They may range from simple on the spot changes involving a piece of equipment to major program reconstructions involving equipment, teaching styles, rules and environmental modifications.

For example:

> As a result of a review of **Fran's** gymnastic program, modifications include colour coded place mats and apparatus, individualised shorter sessions, the arrangement of a rostered buddy system and some changes in the personal support necessary for particular elements of the program.

Ad hoc modifications occur *while* an activity or program is happening. They may be made on the spot as the teacher/instructor reviews what is happening and makes a decision to change an aspect of the activity for the benefit of the individual and group.

For example:

> During an Aussie Footy game **Dave's** teacher decides to change Dave's position on the field to help him become more involved.

Planned modifications generally involve some activity or program meeting beforehand to consider the details of what will actually occur. Ideally, all modifications are planned ahead of time. This is not reality, however, and often ongoing modifications need to be incorporated into activities and programs.

Minor modifications occur where the change is straightforward and immediate to implement. They may be planned over a series of like activities or be a one-off, specific to a singular activity. While a modification may be minor it may also be highly significant for the individual.

For example:

> **Joanne** recommends to her coach that she uses an alternative and readily available light bat during softball, improving her grip and enhance her ability to participate independently.

Major modifications are sometimes necessary, particularly in relation to the inclusion of people with high support needs. These, again, may be to a particular activity or program and may be ad hoc or planned in advance.

For example:

> **Jane's** parents, teachers and integration aides meet at the beginning of term to discuss the implications of Jane's shunt on physical activity. They design a range of alternative activities for certain parts of the program to avoid any potential damage to the shunt during particular activities.

Activities or **programs** may be modified. A program is a planned sequential series of activities constructed specifically for a particular goal. An activity is a component part of the program. Activities and programs are separated here, as this helps to isolate the differences between the inclusion process for singular activities and a collective sequence of planned activities.

It is possible to participate across a number of stages of the inclusion process. For example, Stephen could:

- represent his school in table tennis and compete in tournaments that are exclusively for young people with disabilities

- specialise in table tennis yet also compete in other sports such as basketball and archery that require some modification.

1.7 Terminology

> 'Other people's attitudes and comments can often make us feel disabled in a way that the disability itself does not. Most of us, on a daily and continuing basis, are reminded that we are seen as different and it is this loss of anonymity in a crowd that we regret so keenly.'
>
> Morris (1989) 73

While there are no hard and fast rules about what should and should not be said when referring to people with disabilities there are a few accepted terms that do attempt to break down some of the social stigmas associated with disability. As a general rule it is appropriate to use words and expressions that put the person ahead of the disability. For example:

☑ **person with a disability or disabilities**
☒ disabled, handicapped, spastic or crippled

☑ **person who has**
☒ crippled by, afflicted with, suffering from, victim of

☑ **person who uses a wheelchair**
☒ confined, bound, restricted to or dependent on

☑ **person with an intellectual disability**
☒ retarded, mentally retarded, backward

☑ **person who is deaf, hard of hearing**
☒ *deaf and dumb, deaf mute*

☑ **person with a behavioural or emotional disorder, child who has autism**
☒ *mental patient, mentally ill, mental, insane*

☑ **person with a learning disability**
☒ *learning disabled, learning difficulty, difficult*

It is not so important what is said in many circumstances but how it is said and who it is said to. Certainly, when modelling accepted terminology the person-first rule is a good guideline. If in doubt ask the parent, guardian or person with a disability about appropriate terminology.

> 'All I needed was someone to tell me I was doing well. But even thinking about the school plays, the parts they gave me were all highlighting my disability. Once I had the part of Long John Silver, the sea captain with one leg. The teacher had given me a real blunderbuss to put in my pocket. Then at the most important part of the play I had to draw the blunderbuss out and say 'back, back, you mutinous mob.'
>
> David Swift: in Humphries and Gordon (1992) 55

Section 2
Getting ready for school

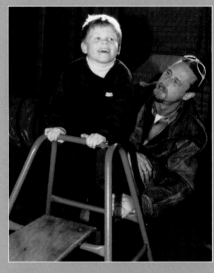

Contents

2.1 Adapting and modifying physical activity at school — **28**

2.1.1 Active Australia Schools Network — 28

2.1.2 Inclusion in the school environment — 28

2.1.3 The Golden Rule of Inclusion — 30

2.1.4 How do I go about planning for individual needs? — 32

2.1.5 Developing a planning model — 42

2.1.6 Abilities-based assessment — 47

2.2 Running inclusive activities — **49**

2.2.1 Early childhood to lower primary — 49

2.2.2 Primary — 56

2.2.3 Secondary to post-compulsory — 64

2.2.4 Young people with high support needs — 69

2.2.5 Young people with degenerative conditions — 74

'Accepting me as I am is the first step in our working together'

Lisa Lorens

I am a very intelligent person, but it is hard to express and demonstrate that, so people treat you as though you are dumb because you appear that way to everybody else.

One of my best friends, Christa Dudley, introduced me to athletics when I was just 12. I started at Woden Little Athletics and went in all events. The first year there I won the Best and Fairest.

After Little Athletics, I joined Weston Creek Athletics Club. This was different from Little Athletics because I didn't win all the events. It was here that I learned that I had to train really hard if I wanted to get better. My Mum still says that I spent more time playing in the shrubbery near the track than concentrating on my events. Luckily I did get better and was selected to go to the Pacific School Games in Darwin in 1992 where I won 6 gold and 2 silver medals.

I first got to travel overseas when I was 16 and won silver in the 200m and long jump. I was really happy to be selected in the Paralympic team in 1996, but also sad that I had to give up my other sport, gymnastics. When I got the scholarship at the Australian Institute of Sport, I was also disappointed that I had to give up high jump, shot put, discus and hurdles. Luckily I can occasionally compete in these events for my club at Interclubs.

The people at my club are really nice and now my fellow squad members from the Australian Institute of Sport, Murray, Anton and Trish, also compete as members of my club.

I really want to be the best in the world. My coach and my Mum are almost as determined as I am to achieve this.

2.1 Adapting and modifying physical activity at school

2.1.1 Active Australia Schools Network

Throughout this section reference will be made to the Active Australia Schools Network. The Active Australia Schools Network is a national network of schools committed to developing, supporting and promoting sport and physical activity which is:

- fun
- safe
- challenging
- rewarding
- well managed
- focused on learning
- linked to the community, and
- **inclusive of people with disabilities**

There are many benefits of membership of the Schools Network, not least the support you will get in areas of professional development, resource material and, importantly, links to other schools and community organisations who are dealing with similar issues. Membership of the network is not difficult and will help your school get support. You can register to become a part of the network by photocopying and filling out the form in Appendix 3 and returning it to the National Coordinator marked on the form.

2.1.2 Inclusion in the school environment

Inclusive programming in the school setting basically means that individual needs are met through curriculum adaptations and the provision of appropriate support. Many inclusive programs have succeeded with a commonsense approach but, as someone once said, 'if common sense were so common we'd all have it!'

Young people with disabilities can be active participants in sport and physical activity. In fact, in many cases students can be included with little or no changes to the activities already selected for inclusion into the program and certainly in keeping with the overall goals of the PE or sport program.

For other students, more obvious modifications to the existing activities will be necessary to enable them to participate as fully as possible in the program. The 'level' that the student fits into is not so important. What matters more is which option is most appropriate to enable the student to participate to their fullest ability.

Depending on the individual it may be beneficial for the student to be involved in 'segregated' or 'parallel' activities either on a short or long term basis. This may involve conducting concurrent activities within a session, or additional sessions outside of the regular classes.

Students may have insufficient social skills to participate effectively in a team activity where the focus is on developing and practising team strategies. They could be encouraged to work in small group situations to develop these skills before becoming fully involved in a game situation with the whole class.

For example:

> *Basketball — student will work in small groups during class session; teacher in special education unit may take the student for additional sessions and encourage the development of appropriate social skills.*

A student with multiple disabilities using an electric wheelchair (high support needs) may perform a comparable skill suitable to their ability level.

For example:

> (a) *shotput, javelin or discus — as an alternative use the bean bag (previously an internationally recognised event for people with cerebral palsy). This event involves throwing a beanbag at a circular target (like an archery target) that has been placed on the ground. The beanbag is light and easy to grip and throw.*
>
> (b) *high jump, long jump — due to the use of the electric wheelchair, there are no alternative activities which are beneficial or comparable for this student. The teacher may select a challenging activity that could be performed in the same activity area and utilising similar 'athletic' skills, eg a slalom course.*

A student may participate in all of the activities in the program except those that are considered unsafe for the young person with a disability.

For example:

> *Students with detached retina, hydrocephalus, or atlantoaxial instability etc should avoid activities — such as heading the ball — that place undue stress on the head and/or neck. Allow the students to kick or catch the ball instead.*

2.1.3 The Golden Rule of Inclusion

When modifying the activity or program it is important that the teacher ensures fair participation of all students, ie students with disabilities as well as able-bodied students. Balance needs to be maintained between maximising each student's potential for involvement and achievement, and maintaining the integrity of the activity. By this we mean that minimal changes should be made to the activity so that it is meaningful and challenging for all the class and its purpose is not lost through unnecessary modifications.

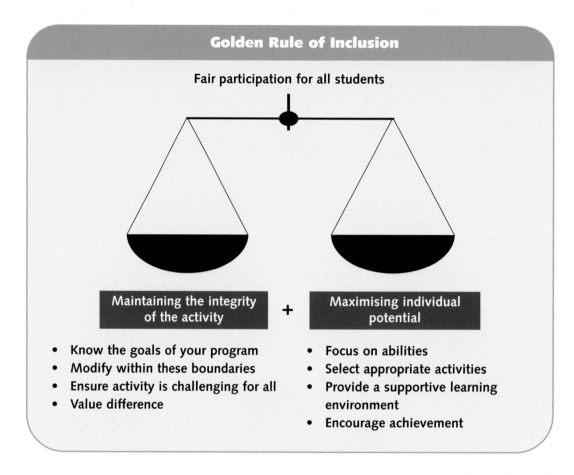

Golden Rule of Inclusion

Fair participation for all students

| Maintaining the integrity of the activity | **+** | Maximising individual potential |

- Know the goals of your program
- Modify within these boundaries
- Ensure activity is challenging for all
- Value difference

- Focus on abilities
- Select appropriate activities
- Provide a supportive learning environment
- Encourage achievement

To maintain the integrity of the activity or program...

Know the goals of your program

- Know which aspects of the program are important for the whole class, ie aspects of the program that are inflexible and must be kept intact.

- Know where you can be flexible with your program.

Modify the activities in keeping with the goals of the program

- Be flexible and not afraid to modify within these boundaries.

- Adapt the program to include suitable activities, or modifications to elements of the activity eg rules, equipment etc.

- Will the integrity of the activity be affected if I change the type of bat, introduce a new zoning rule, or introduce a 'new' sport in the place of a 'traditional' one?

- Provide alternatives if needed for the student with disabilities.

Challenge all the students

- Could these modifications in fact help other able-bodied students in the class as well as students with disabilities to participate more fully? Most likely 'Yes!'
- Introducing new activities or different ways of participating in the same activity can challenge all students.

Encourage students to value difference

- Encourage all students to experiment with different equipment, rules etc to find what suits them best.
- Encourage students to set the rules to enable fair participation for all.
- Use role models (eg Paralympians as well as Olympians).

To maximise the individual's potential...

Focus on the student's abilities

- Focus on what the student *can do* — range of motion, degree of strength, which is their 'best' side etc.
- Ask the student to demonstrate their skills.
- A basic knowledge of their disability, in particular how it affects their physical functioning and safety issues in relation to activities, is important.
- To gauge the individual's current ability and potential, contact the student themselves as well as relevant others. As previously outlined, ask a number of people so that you develop a balanced viewpoint — individuals including the student themselves may have an unrealistic expectation (either too high or low) in relation to their abilities.

Select appropriate activities

- Select activities that will be appropriate for involvement post-school and long term. For students with more limited employment options, use of leisure time and maintenance of health will be a key focus.
- Look at likes and dislikes.
- Set challenging and realistic goals in consultation with others.

Provide a supportive learning environment

- Make the activity as inviting as possible, so that the student is sure to 'Give it a go!'
- Provide opportunities for students to participate at their own level and pace and to achieve appropriate and realistic goals.
- Allow opportunity to practice skills. Sometimes additional time is needed to master skills.
- 'Circuit' activities provide opportunities for student choice, and enable students to work at their own pace.
- A stable physical environment will encourage independence (ie keeping equipment in the same place).
- Encourage students to work together.

Encourage achievement

- Just like able-bodied students, young people with disabilities can achieve incredible physical feats, given the motivation and practice.

- Use role models (Paralympians are role models for all children).

- Look at standards. As a guide you may wish to find out what state and national records or performances exist for athletes with a particular type and level of disability. You may find in fact that you have students at your school who appear to struggle with the traditional curriculum but excel in sports that maximise their potential by focusing on their abilities.

2.1.4 How do I go about planning for individual needs?

One of the first steps in the planning process is to clearly map where your school is at in terms of its readiness to fully embrace students with disabilities. Is the school environment suitable? What is the school ethos and culture? How will they affect the school's ability to accept students with disabilities? These are all important questions that need to be addressed. The good news is this need not be a difficult task. The Active Australia Schools Network guide will assist. The guide encourages you to look at your current physical activity policies and to refocus attention where necessary. It is divided into three categories: school environment/ethos, curriculum teaching and learning, and school community links.

By using the guide in the School Environment/Ethos category your school can identify its readiness in terms of providing a supportive environment for students with disabilities.

Table 1: School environment/ethos

Objective: Our school will provide a supportive environment for all members of the school and the local community to be physically active.

OUR STRENGTHS/ACHIEVEMENTS

Members of school generally supportive of students with disabilities. Some students competed in carnival. Able-bodied students generally encourage students with disabilities. Physical access OK

AREAS FOR IMPROVEMENT	ACTIONS
Need Committee representation. Training for all staff in disability awareness needed.	Form Committee to deal with disability issues. Organise 'Willing and Able' workshop for all staff.

A full blank copy of this form is in Appendix 4. Once you are confident the school has an environment conducive to the inclusion of students with disabilities, you are in a position to take action on the mechanics of the planning process. There are some fundamental guidelines that will help in the planning process. These include:

1. Be prepared to adapt activities

A great misconception about inclusive programming is that young people with disabilities should fit into the existing program and that all students should be treated the same, regardless of different levels of ability.

Teachers regularly allow for individual differences of able-bodied students. The process for modifying activities for students with disabilities is basically the same.

In some instances the activities used for the regular activity session will not be suitable for an inclusive program. In this case the session will need to be adapted to suit the individual needs of the student.

For example:

> **Rahul** *may be prohibited from performing activities in a typical gymnastics tumbling session. Rahul may, however, be able to work on activities that have the same physical education aim of movement control by performing rolls sideways from stomach to back. In this way all students work toward the same goals but in different ways.*

In many cases very simple adaptations or modifications can be made that will allow greater participation by young people with disabilities in physical activity. Every effort should be made to remain as close as possible to the original activity format.

The selection for activities and the level of participation will depend on a number of factors:

- the objectives of the program
- the abilities of the students
- space
- time
- available equipment and facilities.

While all these factors are important, knowing something about the abilities of the individual before programming will make planning more effective in the long term. Most importantly, it will inform the teacher about adaptations required for the inclusive program. Some simple activity adaptations that could be included in an inclusive program are presented in Table 2.

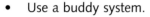

Table 2: General activity adaptations

1 TEACHING STRATEGIES

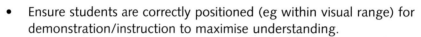

- Make small groups of similar abilities — this allows for individual progress at different levels.

- Make large groups of differing abilities.

- Use game activities for specific purposes such as cardiovascular endurance, coordination, balance.

- Use a buddy system.

- Ensure students are correctly positioned (eg within visual range) for demonstration/instruction to maximise understanding.

- Use visual aids and demonstrations to model the activity.

- Use physical assistance by guiding body parts through a movement.

- Use language that is appropriate to the group.

- Make use of specially designed equipment to assist in learning.

- Always check for understanding of instructions.

- Use 'circuit' activities to allow for students to progress at their own level and pace.

- Introduce 'disabled' sports (activities that may be 'new' for all students and particularly appropriate for the student/s with disabilities).

2 RULES/GAMES STRUCTURE

- Allow for more bounces in a game such as tennis or table tennis.

- Allow for the ball to be hit any number of times in sports such as volleyball.

- Substitute players regularly.

- Allow runners for cricket, softball.

- Use a stationary ball instead of a pitched one, eg use a T-ball batting tee for cricket.

- Have a greater number of players on a team to reduce the amount of activity required by each player.

- Have fewer players to allow freedom of movement.

- Reduce the competitive element.

- Vary time restrictions on games (eg use 'quarters' instead of 'halves') and adapt warm-ups/cool-downs as necessary.

- Use an 'interchange' rule to allow for short periods of exercise and appropriate periods of rest.

(continued next page)

Table 2: General activity adaptations (continued)

- Allow different levels of point scoring, eg in basketball — one point for close to the basket and two or three points for further away.
- Change running to walking.
- Change running/skipping to wheeling/rolling.
- Allow sitting/lying/kneeling instead of standing.
- Try bouncing, rolling or using the underarm toss instead of the overarm throw.

3 ENVIRONMENT

- Reduce the size of the court or playing area for soccer, hockey, tennis, basketball, rugby.
- Use smooth/indoor surface rather than grass.
- Ensure court markings contrast well with the surrounding environment.
- Lower the nets for badminton, volleyball.
- Use zones within the playing area or court.
- Be aware of the lighting, natural or artificial, and its effect on an individual's ability to track movement and objects.
- Minimise distractions in the surrounding area.

4 EQUIPMENT

- Use lighter bats or racquets and/or shorter handles.
- Use lighter, bigger, slower bouncing balls or even balls with bells in.
- Use equipment that contrasts with the playing area background, eg fluoro ball on dark court or white markers on grass.

KEY POINTS

- As skill levels increase, adaptations may need to be changed to allow for a continued development in skill acquisition.

- Rather than make these modifications just for the students with disabilities, allow all students to do a modified program such as T-ball — allow all students to select an appropriate ball and striking implement when hitting. These simple modifications may also help other students who may have difficulties with the regular activity and provide new challenges for students who normally participate at a high level.

CHECKLIST TO DETERMINE THE APPROPRIATENESS OF ADAPTATIONS	Y/N
• Will the adaptation increase the child's participation in the activity?	
• Does the adaption allow the child to participate in an activity that is preferred by the child or his/her family and peers?	
• Will the adaptation be useful later in life and allow participation in community programs?	
• Will the adaptation take less time to teach than teaching the skill directly?	
• Does the adaptation require specialist use and technical support and maintenance?	
• Will using the adaptation mean related communication and/or motor skills will be enhanced?	

The AUSSIE SPORT modified sports program promotes some 43 modified games, many of which are suitable for young people with disabilities.

Disability-specific activities

For some students with disabilities, traditional activities may present some barriers to participation. While many of these barriers to participation can be overcome through modifying components of the activity, another solution is to consider selecting a disability-specific activity, ie one that has been specifically developed for people with a disability. Many of these sports are played at Paralympic level.

Selecting such activities will not only allow students with disabilities to participate to their fullest ability, it will also allow able-bodied students who are very competent at regularly selected sports to be challenged in a new and interesting way. These new activities may be also very suitable for other able-bodied students who may not usually excel at traditional sports. Examples include goalball, boccia, wheelchair rugby, wheelchair basketball and sitting volleyball.

These sports are just as appropriate for meeting the goals of the PE program in relation to development of skills, fitness as well as teamwork, leadership, social skills etc.

Taking wheelchair basketball as an example, there are several ways in which disability specific sports could be included in the PE program:

- as the sole focus for the term — substituting wheelchair basketball for basketball (skills, drills and the actual game)

- by running concurrently with another activity, ie by using two courts, one for each type. Students can choose either to focus on basketball or wheelchair basketball, or can combine both

- by selecting key aspects of wheelchair basketball to include as part of the regular program (eg skills, drills, lead-up games, the actual game, promotional visit from a team)

- by having the student with disabilities participate in wheelchair basketball skills, drills etc, or by using the relevant alternative rules when playing basketball with the rest of the class.

For details of these sports see Contacts/Help.

2. Allow for appropriate support

One of the problems of early attempts at mainstreaming was that young people with disabilities tended to be 'dumped' into the regular class situation without appropriate support.

The success of inclusion depends very much on adopting a team work approach. This is particularly important where young people with high support needs are included in program planning. Where a young person is integrated into the regular school system from an environment that has provided a wide range of supports, it is important that a comparable level of support is provided in the regular setting. Supports would have included equipment, special instruction and personnel such as volunteers, assistance and/or education specialists.

Allowing for appropriate support will require collaboration with a range of individuals who, at some stage, are responsible for the provision of services that affect the lives of young people with disabilities. These individuals may not be directly associated with the school setting. They could be parents, community groups, the social services or from a therapeutic/medical setting. On occasions specialist personnel can join in activities and assist the teacher during the early part of the program.

For example:

> *A physiotherapist joins in the Wednesday afternoon session, arriving before activities begin to administer stretch therapy for* **Stephen**. *The teacher gradually learns the basic techniques of stretch therapy applicable for Stephen over a number of weeks until the skills are mastered and the physiotherapist no longer needs to attend on a regular basis.*

In terms of dependence, young people with high support needs only differ from their able-bodied peers to the extent that they rely on others for assistance. Wherever possible ascertain from the student what type and level of assistance is needed.

Assistance should not mean the young person with a disability assumes a subordinate or helpless role; rather, that he/she is able to participate as independently as possible in the activity.

The meaning of independence also needs to be considered in the context of providing support. Independence should not mean that young people with disabilities do everything themselves. Independence means that assistance is provided when and how the individual requires it. The individual should be able to choose when and how that assistance takes place.

When planning for support, ascertain how much is required and ask yourself if that level of assistance is required on an ongoing basis? It may be that the level of support can be reduced over time as skills and independence develop.

In many areas of academic functioning, physically impaired students are reliant on others (most often teacher aides rather than teachers) to help them complete tasks in the classroom setting. Often this guidance does not follow the same procedure as instruction to a student without physical impairment.

On many occasions the student is guided, both in thinking and performance, by an adult, employing adult reasoning, influenced and shaped by years of experience. In such instances the student is required to passively accept previously unencountered concepts, and indeed whole chunks of information as being correct, without having first hand experience.

The result is...It is perceived the student understands the concept or has the skill, upon 'successful' completion of an activity.

The question is...How much of the activity was guided or even completed by the adult and how much was done by the student?

Appendix 5 has a tool which can help teachers to monitor this balance in the teaching/learning situation.

Some tried and tested support systems include:

- **Team teaching**

    Two or more teachers instruct the class together in a class that includes young people with disabilities. This frees a teacher to work on a one-to-one basis with any student.

- **Role models**

    Providing young people with the opportunity to watch 'similar others' perform activities to a high level gives young people, not just those with disabilities, greater confidence and expectations that they too can aspire to such a level. Remember, Paralympians are role models for all children.

- **Peer and cross-age tutoring**

    Peer tutoring refers to calling on class peers to assist with instruction. There are benefits for all students in this situation as they work together toward activity goals.

Be careful to match students appropriately in terms of skill levels and aptitude. Cross-age tutoring works in basically the same way as peer tutoring, with older students assisting and instructing peers during the program.

- **Parents and volunteers**

  Parents and volunteers may be able to contribute significantly to the individualisation of the PE or sport program. Involving parents provides many benefits, not least providing the young person who has a disability with the opportunity to translate skills learnt in the educational setting to the home setting. The parents may not be the parents of the young person with the disability.

3. Empower the individual with the ability to make choices

Providing children with disabilities with the opportunity to make decisions about their physical education programming has several advantages. The young person can suggest ways to help the teacher adapt equipment, make rule modifications or change the play environment to suit their particular needs. He/she may also help you to think a bit more laterally about various options.

This needs to be done without jeopardising the integrity of the activity or excluding able-bodied peers. It empowers the student to gain a sense of ownership of the program and to assume a degree of responsibility and control over their own physical well-being. Again, this is particularly important for children with intellectual disabilities and behavioural type conditions, as they are often denied any input into decisions about their lives. Keep in mind that, on occasions, limited choice is the best and most appropriate action for some young people.

4. Be realistic in choosing placements — use the 'law of natural proportions'!

Statistics on disability suggest that 10–15% of school age children have some type of disability. The 'law of natural proportions' means that the placement of young people with disabilities into physical education or sport programs follows the normal ratio of young people with and without disabilities in the community.

It would be quite normal for 2–3 individuals with disabilities to be included in a group of 20–30 young people. Using the law of natural proportions makes inclusion much more manageable for the teacher, particularly when young people with high support needs are included. Do not use the 'law' as a reason to exclude a young person from activity.

5. Make sure activities are age appropriate

Chronological age of the child should be the main yardstick when planning an inclusive program. Some programs have relied on functional age classification as the criteria for program design. Most sport programs are designed specifically as sequential motor development programs.

Children with disabilities should be allowed the opportunity to progress through the same motor development patterns as their same-age peers.

Ensure that you are planning for success and that the activities are appropriate to the skill levels of the children. This does not necessarily mean winning but could mean achieving a 'PB' in the long jump or making a set number of baskets in a modified game of basketball.

6.   Develop functional skills

This refers to developing the skills that are required in everyday life, and for future years.

For example:

> *Pushing a wheelchair is a functional skill that is required in everyday life whereas throwing a beanbag to a partner is not something expected outside the school playground. The teacher has to judge what is important for the child at a certain age given their ability.*

This is, of course, related to the age appropriateness concept mentioned above. It may mean adapting traditional games or altering the program to accommodate children with and without disabilities in the same activity. This does not mean that an activity cannot be run simply because it is fun and a challenge.

7.   Develop school community links

Wherever possible activities should be run in their most natural environment. For primary school children the regular setting includes the school playground, the regular physical education class or the local facility. For secondary school children it may mean the local bowling alley or swimming pool. This is particularly important for children with intellectual disabilities or with conditions such as autism and schizophrenia, since these children often have difficulty generalising skills learnt in one environment to other environments.

Collaboration with the local community is vital. It is vital because the work that is done with the student with a disability in the school setting can often be undone in the community when the student leaves the school. School community links foster acceptance and awareness of the needs of young people with disabilities.

The Active Australia Schools Network guide category 3 is specifically designed to assist the school in promoting and providing for physical activity in collaboration with the local community.

Table 3: School community links

Objective: Our school will promote and provide for physical activity in collaboration with the local community.

OUR STRENGTHS/ACHIEVEMENTS

Good relationship with wheelchair sports. Previous visits by disability groups and spine safe organisations. Local boccia club uses school facilities

AREAS FOR IMPROVEMENT	ACTIONS
Need more joint initiatives with local disability sport groups. No staff skills to assist with coaching in specific modified sports.	Establish contact with local disability sport groups. Organise Coaching Athletes with Disabilities Course for school staff.

A full blank copy of the form is at Appendix 6.

8. Adapt only when necessary

Adaptations to teaching style, rules, environments and equipment should be made only when necessary. They should be minimal and, where appropriate, can be temporary. As far as possible, they should not affect the integrity of the activity. Adaptations can mean physical assistance through a 'buddy' system, through adapted equipment or through modified rules or game situations (see Tables 1 and 2).

For example:

Children being given brightly coloured bibs for a team game of tag where **Nicholas** *is included.*

Individualised physical education should allow the child with a disability to participate as independently as possible in age appropriate, functional activities in the most natural settings.

2.1.5 Developing a planning model

Research and anecdotal evidence tell us that children typically spend only about 25% of their lesson time actually doing the activity. The rest of their time is made up of waiting for something to happen, being involved in organising the lesson, listening to instructions and so on. Teachers, similarly, only spend about 30% of their time actually instructing. Clearly, the need for planning is crucial to quality teaching, whether this includes young people with disabilities or not.

Even within the same group, young people experience physical activity in different ways. Unfortunately, often the perceived success of physical activity lessons is judged by the apparent involvement of the group as a whole. The true success can more effectively be judged by the involvement and learning experience of each individual child.

For example:

> *Some children with disabilities could be described as 'competent bystanders' where they become skilled at avoiding participation. Others experience physical activity as an intimidating environment where their physical and/or intellectual characteristics are continually on display. These children may leave the lesson feeling inadequate or in some way alienated from the group. Could the group lesson in this circumstance be described as a success?*

Individualising your program will help avoid these isolated negative experiences. It will improve the performances of all your children and enable you to measure the effectiveness of your program more accurately. Individualised planning is simply an example of 'good practice' in physical education — it is not a process specifically geared to disability and does not necessarily mean one-to-one instruction.

The following table presents a step-by-step approach to planning for inclusion. Be flexible and be prepared to adapt to circumstances as they occur. Involve a range of individuals in the planning process, such as other teachers, parents, 'special' educators and child therapists. You will need to adapt it to suit your particular circumstances.

Table 4: Planning for inclusion

AREA	COMMENTS
Implement appropriate policy and curriculum practices Identify 'readiness' of school culture/ethos. Take action to foster inclusive culture.	
Determine what to teach Assess present level of performance. Set short and long-term objectives.	
Examine the regular physical education curriculum Which present activities match individual needs (use 'activity'/'task' analysis)? Which present activities do not match the individual needs but are important for the student? Which present activities are inappropriate?	
Determine adaptations needed in the regular curriculum How often will the student receive instruction? Where will the student receive instruction? How will the student be prepared for instruction? What instructional modifications are required? What equipment adaptations are required? Will adaptations allow the specific learning objectives outlined in the relevant PE syllabus to be met? How will performance be assessed?	
Determine the level of support needed for your program Base this on type of activities and abilities of student. Use the 'inclusion process' to determine appropriateness.	
Prepare yourself for instruction Discuss the amount of support that will be required. Discuss the availability of consultation with special education teachers and/or adapted physical education specialists. Ensure the needs of all the students are provided for. Remember your workload will not necessarily increase if the program is planned properly.	

(continued next page)

Table 4: Planning for inclusion (continued)	
AREA	**COMMENTS**
Prepare all students for inclusion Talk about students with disabilities in general; use videos that emphasise abilities. Role play various types of disabilities. Invite guest speakers with disabilities to your class. Take students to a special school or better still to the school of the student to be included to meet him/her. Talk about the student to be included, emphasising abilities. Discuss ways the students can help the student with a disability.	
Prepare support personnel Discuss specific student with whom they will working. Discuss the student's physical education program. Discuss personnel responsibilities. Discuss to whom they can go if they have questions.	

(Adapted from Block 1994: 50)

Develop your planning model so that records of student achievement meet, as far as possible, the relevant learning outcomes outlined in the relevant PE syllabus.

Implement appropriate policy and curriculum practices

Initially, your school may need to develop and implement policies and curriculum practices that reflect the importance and benefits of physical activity for students with disabilities. Again, the Active Australia Schools Network guide category 2 can assist with identifying what policies and practices may need to be developed.

Table 5: Curriculum teaching and learning

Objective: Our school will develop and implement policies and curriculum practices that reflect the importance and benefits of physical activity.

OUR STRENGTHS/ACHIEVEMENTS

All staff encourage students with disabilities as much as possible. Staff work with carers and other support workers in a cooperative manner. Successfully ran disability sports Paralympic day

AREAS FOR IMPROVEMENT	ACTIONS
Need to develop a Disability Action Plan/Policy.	Establish committee to direct policy document and provide staff training.

A full blank copy of the form is at Appendix 7.

Determine what to teach

- What skills are needed in his/her current and future physical education setting?
- What motor skills are required?
- What are the child's interests?
- What are the parents' interests?
- What do the child's peers do in the same class?
- What are the child's strengths and weaknesses — record child's abilities according to their basic individual motor needs (refer to Table 6).
- Set goals for completion of first term instructional objectives and first year goals in line with known learning outcomes.
- What will the child be doing at upper primary level?
- Are goals realistic and achievable?

Examine the regular physical education curriculum

- What activities currently take place?
- Try creating a 'daily routine chart' that will help incorporate the child's short and long-term goals.
- Discuss the child's individual needs and abilities with parents, therapists and/or other teachers.
- Are there some activities that appear to be either developmentally or physically inappropriate to the child's needs?
- Do certain activities need modification and/or adaptation?
- What are the basic goals of your program? Do they match the child's needs?

Determine adaptations

- What is the child's timetable — how often is individualised instruction possible?

- Can other teachers contribute to broad movement goals?

- Is professional help necessary/available, and can the regular teachers learn from such help?

- Will breaking down the activity into individual component parts (termed 'task analysis') help determine individual needs? Generally, the lower the level of functional ability, the greater the need for task analysis. Task analysis may, however, play an important role in the individualisation process, regardless of the severity of the condition.

- Where will the child receive instruction? Are separate settings sometimes needed for individual or specialist instruction?

- Do you need to adapt the environment or create stable settings?

- Is the child prepared for inclusion? Is there any physical and/or instructional preparation required? Do you need to meet with child before full inclusion?

- Have certain types of verbal and non-verbal cues been used before with the child that you need to incorporate into your program?

- Are the other children prepared for inclusion — do you need to 'brief' a buddy?

- Are the adaptations determined appropriate to the child's needs?

Determine what support is needed

- How much and for how long will individual support be necessary?

- Who is responsible for implementing the program and what is likely to be the teacher/student ratio?

- Will extra support be needed for individualised instruction? Where is this support likely to come from?

- Can assistance be provided by other children, staff or parents at certain times and for certain activities? Will it be possible to shuffle help between children/staff/ parents as the day progresses? Do you need to timetable 'helpers' to fit into the individual's schedule?

- Will a 'buddy' or 'peer tutor' system be necessary? Will you need to brief/train the peer tutor beforehand?

Prepare other staff for inclusion

- Do you need to bring in special education staff, child therapists or parents to hep train other staff members? Ensure training takes place before inclusion and is ongoing.

- Share any concerns you have with others. People are often only too pleased to offer assistance if asked.

- Do the staff need to meet the child before inclusion so they can better understand his/her particular interests, behaviour and temperament?

- Are specific handling and/or behaviour management techniques required?

- Arrange for special education staff/child therapists to visit the child's new school environment. They will be able to help determine appropriate levels of support required and adaptations needed, including therapy and specific teaching techniques.

- Does the special education teacher/therapist/parent need to accompany the child during the first few days in the new environment?

- Are appropriate in-service courses available in your area?

Implement program and evaluate

- The first few days of transition from one setting to another are important for the staff and even more important for the child. Draw up a simple checklist, based on the answers to the above questions, and consult special education teachers and parents on a regular basis.

- Monitor the individual's progress. Again, initially this may be done in consultation with specialist staff who may visit from time to time to check on progress and to suggest modifications. Plan monthly meetings with specialist staff/parents if required.

2.1.6 Abilities-based assessment

Assessment in physical activity is a requirement for many teachers across the country. Assessment criteria differs from state to state. Two of the perceptions teachers have on this topic are that the 'usual' assessment criteria do not apply to young people with disabilities, and that it is too hard to make this assessment as you need specific (or 'specialist') skills. There is also the difficulty, allied to this, that in making an assessment you are comparing people with a disability to able-bodied norms. Neither perception is correct. The same criteria are possible for all children and you do not need specific skills to do an assessment or to compare young people with disabilities to able-bodied norms.

One way to do this is to focus on identifying the abilities of young people and matching them with some of the skills the activity needs. This is an example of skill assessment. We recognise that assessment takes a much broader focus in the school setting.

Do not underestimate the feedback from the individual with the disability. Often, their personal insights and thoughts about an activity can help identify abilities and likes and dislikes.

Table 6 provides a simple tool to assist you in matching abilities and activity requirements. Note both the skill requirements and the fitness requirements of the activity.

Table 6: Abilities-based assessment form

Abilities-based assessment form   **Name:** Stephen

Activity	Tennis				
Skill	Serve				
Activity requirements	Good balance with large base of support	Eye–hand coordination and accuracy (timing)	Upper body rotation and speed	Racquet manipulation (right angles)	Flow (preparation and follow-through)
Present abilities	Greater mobility down left side of body	Good upper body rotation	Firm grip Good strength on LHS	Enjoys sport and understands requirements	Good eye–hand coordination
Future practice	Balance — increasing base of support	Enhance eye–hand coordination exercises	Enjoyment, fun games	Racquet work, manipulation	

Teachers may wish to seek further information on what constitutes high level performance for students with disabilities when assessing students for Years 10–12 Health and Physical Education (Board Subject). For further information on current state and national records/performances in disability sport, contact the relevant state or national sports organisation for the disabled. See Contacts/help.

2.2   Running inclusive activities

Children are natural explorers. Young children enjoy learning about their bodies and how to control them. Curiosity motivates children to explore new experiences that in turn help enhance and develop the senses of touch, sight, hearing, smell and taste. Physical activity also helps develop young children's balance, strength, coordination and awareness of body parts. Young children with disabilities are no different in their eagerness to explore these new experiences.

2.2.1 Early childhood to lower primary

Multi-sensory activities

Children learn so much through touching, hearing and seeing that we should provide lots of opportunities for them to develop these senses. Start with these easy to organise activities:

- In the bath play with soap, bubbles, sponges, face washers and toys.
- In the backyard or playground, play with a sprinkler or hose with the water just trickling or play in a wading pool.
- In a sandpit, roll in the sand and cover arms and legs, or whole body, with it.
- With a blanket — roll your child up in a blanket, leaving the head exposed.

NB: These activities require adult supervision.

Some suggested adaptations and considerations for our children include:

Stephen Water activities should be safe for Stephen. Ensure the water is lukewarm. Cold water may activate the 'startle' reflex and aggravate spasticity. It may be helpful to lightly massage the right hand and arm first. This will help relax him for the fine motor tasks.

Jane Take advice. It is likely that Jane should not take part in the blanket activities — there is a possibility of dislodging the shunt. Watch for scrapes and sores when playing in sand for long periods, particularly in lower body — she may now be aware of these herself. Make yourself or a colleague available for toileting — water activities may trigger bowel movements.

Nicholas Explain that you will be using water and allow some orientation by touch before play begins. Use brightly coloured toys, face washers etc. Nicholas has some light perception and may be able to locate them independently.

Fran It is not uncommon for children with autism to reject certain sensations of touch. If Fran rejects water or sand, gradually introduce these items for only brief periods of time. Carry out these activities in the same place, using the same playthings each time. Create a routine of going from one activity to another.

Joanne Make sure you use appropriate lifting techniques for getting Joanne in and out of the chair. Do not be over vigorous in activities and watch for bumps and bruises down the left side. Apply appropriate left side support if necessary. (See Appendix 2)

Rahul Supervise carefully during blanket activity; avoid excessive and rough rolling.

Dave Emphasise the fun aspect of these activities. Try to keep the group size small, particularly during the water activities.

Hearing, touch and sight

There are many games you can play with your children that will develop their senses of hearing, touch and sight.

- Hide and seek — the person hiding rings a bell or chants a rhyme so that the finder can follow the sound.

- Have the children cover their eyes with their hands and identify sounds such as saucepan lids banging together, a whistle, a bell. Show the child the object after the identification attempt.

- Make a 'feely' bag or box to hide objects that the child can try to identify by touch.

- Peeking cylinder — cut windows in a cardboard cylinder or box for your child to view pictures pasted on the other side.

Stephen Encourage Stephen to use his right hand to identify objects: allow more time if necessary. Adjust the depth of the picture in the cylinder until Stephen is at least able to make out its basic shape. Do not exclude him from the activity because of his vision impairment; learn to understand what he can see and use that.

Jane Mix up the depth of the visual stimulus and auditory pitch. Do not make visual objects too small and allow Jane to be the 'hider'. During the 'feely' bag game check that Jane is fine to handle latex objects; children with spina bifida can be allergic to latex.

Nicholas For hide and seek make sure that Nicholas is familiar with the environment — the person hiding must stay within the confines of that environment. Use clues, eg you are 'hot' or 'cold'. Do not have too many children playing at one time and make a rule that nobody is allowed to run. Do not change the 'feely' bag for Nicholas's sake. Also, use everyday sounds for hearing games.

Fran Associate sounds with visual images — show Fran a picture of the sound you are making. Make sure it is quiet and distractions are kept to a minimum when other children are playing. Show Fran what she has identified from the 'feely' bag — reinforce her success and repeat the task on the other days.

Joanne Allow places for and enough time for Joanne to hide — if she is the finder make sure all areas are accessible. A buddy may assist but make sure he/she only acts on Joanne's instructions even when she is 'cold'.

Rahul Hearing, touch and sight activities are particularly good for Rahul at an early age. Enlarge pictures in cylinder, if he has problems with recognition. Use a variety of common household and play items for him to identify and ask him what they are used for. His ability to process kinaesthetic information may be poor, so persist, and reward and encourage success.

Dave Make plenty of alternative play items to keep Dave occupied. Try to mix up activities that require different levels of energy input. Use 'feely' bag objects that emit different noises.

Strength

A strong body is important, not only for eventual performance but also for general good health.

- Crab walk — move along the floor on hands and feet with the child's chest facing the ceiling.

- Seal slide — start by lying face down, with hands under the shoulders. Straighten arms to lift upper body off ground. Hands walk forward. Weight is taken through the arms. Ensure that children keep straight and do not sag in the lower back.

- Bear walk — start with the weight on all fours (hands and feet). Child moves one side of the body, then the other. Hands and feet on the one side of the body work as a unit. Lifting from the floor and moving together.

Stephen Incorporate relaxation exercises as part of Stephen's warm-up, concentrating on the right side. Only support if necessary — will probably work out a way of crab, seal and bear walking by himself. It is likely that Stephen's right side extensor muscles are significantly weaker than his flexor muscles, so it is important to work on exercises that promote extension movements, eg encourage him to 'push up' during these exercises.

Jane Jane should be able to perform these activities out of her wheelchair. Upper body strength is important for her. Avoid placing emphasis on her condition. Watch for scrapes on knees especially during seal and bear walks. Encourage lower body 'pushing'.

Nicholas Ensure adequate space between children — move in one direction and to a 'rhythm' (eg clapping or the beat of a drum). Consider a 'tether' between Nicholas and a partner.

Fran Explain activity as succinctly as possible using visual demonstration. Place 'markers' (small mats) on the floor to indicate starting position and make a finishing point.

Joanne Out of the wheelchair, work on resistance exercises while the other children perform walks. Assign a buddy to 'push' against the left arm and leg while sitting.

Rahul Provide physical assistance through back support especially for crab walk. Encourage upper body strength exercises but remember the use of support and a soft working surface.

Dave Rely heavily on visual demonstration. These are fun activities so try to enhance the activity by making up stories about crabs, seals and bears. They can also be quite energetic so monitor any fatigue. In between activities continue the stories to provide continuity and interest.

Body awareness

The following activities and games will help your children to become aware of what their bodies can do.

- Copying games

- Follow me — place your hands on different parts of your body and have the children mirror you. Then give spoken directions, such as 'Put your hand on your head'.

- Sheet game — cover child with a sheet from the chin down. Hold an arm or a leg and ask 'What have I got?' Child tries to name the part of the body.

- Hoop game — ask the child to place it over a part of your body, eg over your head, on your shoulder.

- Ball game — copy where the child places the ball (eg on top of your head, under your arm).

- Tracing the body — use a sheet of paper, such as butcher's paper, and trace around your child's body (or parts of). Both of you can name the parts as you trace.

Stephen Encourage Stephen to use both sides of the body equally. Should be capable of performing all activities well.

Jane Jane's physical condition will have little impact on her ability to perform these tasks. The tracing game is particularly good in terms of developing positive body image. Encourage and applaud the identification of specific body parts — do not ignore the lower body. Reinforce the positive 'whole body' image.

Nicholas Copying games are very valuable for Nicholas. Give precise instructions on what you are doing — have the other children try the 'follow me' game with their eyes closed. Don't forget spoken feedback for Nicholas — he'll want to know if he got it right!

Fran Visual demonstrations are important for Fran. Manually guide (not place) Fran for various body parts. Try watching a 'couple' do it first then manually guide through the task using only minimum instruction (be sure to repeat the located part). Perhaps use a 'picture' to show parts that need to be identified.

Joanne Her physical condition should not have any significant effect on her ability to perform the tasks. Rely more on visual demonstration than spoken instruction. Do not ignore affected body parts.

Rahul All these activities are suitable for Rahul and need no adaptation.

Dave All these activities are suitable for Dave and need no adaptation.

Obstacle courses

Obstacle courses are great fun for children of all ages. You can make courses indoors and outdoors, using everyday objects.

You could include some of the following in your course:

- footsteps placed on the floor
- carpet squares
- ropes for climbing up and down
- objects to crawl over, under and through
- shoe boxes to step into

Changing the obstacles, and changing how the children move through the course, can make it harder or easier. Try different ways of moving through the course — such as walking, crawling, jumping, running and hopping.

Stephen Stephen will be able to negotiate and learn from all kinds of obstacle courses. Be aware that 'crawl through' activities should be wide enough for all children, that balance beams should be challenging yet wide enough so that Stephen is required to work on weight transfer and compensation movements.

Jane Do not make the course very long. Set up the course so that Jane can get around in her wheelchair or with the use of crutches. Create 'alternative' routes so that the integrity of the activity is not affected for all children.

Nicholas Paint the obstacles bright colours. Try attaching small bells where obstacles begin. Ensure objects are soft and there are no sharp protruding edges.

Fran Structure the course with firm lines and routes. Ensure there is a clear start and end. Try creating stations where children must stop before moving onto the next part. Do not change the course too often and reward Fran each time the course is completed successfully.

Joanne Alternative routes on the same course will allow Joanne to negotiate the same course with the help of a buddy if required. Set the course up on a flat surface and make obstacles that she can duck under and weave around.

Rahul Do not create high obstacles that Rahul may fall off. Ensure all ground areas are padded. With new courses let Rahul follow a buddy slowly around first.

Dave Try to gauge the obstacles that will challenge Dave yet also allow him a good chance for success. Avoid obstacles that require fine balance and coordination skills. Obstacle courses are 'outgoing' group activities. Be aware that Dave may react poorly to this, but try to encourage confidence and self-esteem.

Relaxation

It is a good idea to end each activity session with some form of relaxation. It might help to block out extra light or sounds. Have children listen to or focus on one stimulus (eg their breathing, a distant bell, traffic, birds, dogs).

Have children lie down on their stomachs — cover them with a sheet or blanket (let them choose whether to cover their heads or not). Roll a beach ball over them or knead them with a tennis ball.

- Have the children breathe deeply for a short while. Check, by moving their limbs, that they are actually relaxing.

- Pretend to be a rag doll or a floppy clown.

- Imagine being an ice-cream melting.

- Guided imagery — have the children lie on their backs with eyes closed and relaxed. Talk them through an imaginary situation, such as lying on the beach under an umbrella, or being a parachute floating through the air.

Stephen   Performing relaxation exercises is especially important and valuable for Stephen. Try to work with Stephen independently on these. Spasticity may be reduced by holding the spastic body part in patterns opposite to those of the dominating spastic patterns. A common relaxation technique used by therapists is called rotation. With Stephen lying on his back, gently bend the hips and knees toward the body with your hands on Stephen's knees. Slowly and gently move both legs as a unit to the left, and then to the right. Repeat until you feel the body relax. Consult a professional about suitable relaxation exercises.

Jane   Ask Jane if she would like to relax out of the wheelchair, free of braces and crutches. Use 'crash mats' or cushions to lie on.

Nicholas   Ensure that you explain clearly what is about to happen. With guided imagery describe your situation well.

Fran   Try not to program activities that are very active immediately before relaxation periods. Have regular relaxation sessions and assign Fran her own space. Use calming music if available.

Joanne   Ask Joanne if she would like to relax out of her wheelchair.

Rahul   Work with Rahul individually while guiding the class through relaxation tasks. Do not 'knead' very hard and keep him warm, especially on colder days.

Dave   Include some food reward (jelly beans are good) after relaxation periods and before further exercise. Make sure all the children get some reward, not just Dave. Try to gauge the regularity of relaxation periods for Dave.

2.2.2 Primary

Experts agree on the importance of providing rich, stimulating motor experiences for young children. Enhancing and expanding the movement vocabulary of a young child is just as important as improving word and reading vocabularies. Since movement is the child's first language, a variety of experiences will help make the language as precise and expressive as possible.

Children need, therefore, the opportunity to experience and explore, not only to find out what they can do, but also what they can't do. They need a chance to make mistakes and to learn from them. They need the chance to build on the skills they have already acquired, by moving on to more challenging activities as they master the early ones.

The body in motion (6–8 years)

Controlled movement is a skill that is acquired through practice. The following activities help children to discover the capabilities of their bodies and to build up their movement skills. Safety is very important. Make sure that the play area is clear and free from obstructions, including wheelchairs and assistive devices not being used.

Small group games and activities

Tag

- Chain tag — one child is designated to be 'it' and on 'go' attempts to catch or tag another player. When caught, the children hold hands and chase the next child. Each child caught joins the chain. Only the players at the end of the chain can tag a free player.

- Freeze tag — when children run to avoid being tagged by 'it'. If tagged the child must remain motionless until a team mate frees him/her by touching.

- Tunnel tag — where a tagged child must stand with feet apart until freed by a team mate who crawls between their feet.

Stephen   Restrict the size of the playing area so that when Stephen is 'it' he will be able to corner other players. Create additional rules — for example, all other children have to 'hop'. Make a time limit for being 'it'. Because of elimination factor in both freeze tag and tunnel tag, slower children may spend time waiting to be freed rather than running. Imposing a time limit so that chasers and fleers change roles regularly allows the slower children to gain time running.

Jane   Try modifications that slow the game down, such as other children hopping, all children having partners, or rule that only walking is allowed. Ensure that the game is played on a suitable surface if Jane is in her wheelchair.

Nicholas   Have the one who is 'it' wear a brightly coloured bib and/or carry bells so Nicholas can detect when 'it' is close. Give Nicholas a buddy, ensure the play area is free of other obstacles and ask the other children not to run into him during play. Make a rule that you must verbally signal when tagged. Freeze and tunnel tag are more appropriate than chain tag for Nicholas.

Fran   Accompany Fran during game; associate 'tag' with 'stop' or 'run'. Restrict the size of the group and the playing area. Mark clear boundaries.

Joanne   Use 'slowing' tactics mentioned above. Use hard surface and warn other children about running into the wheelchair.

Rahul   Make a friendly and cooperative environment and try to reinforce that being 'it' does not mean a 'lesser' role to play in the game.

Dave   Tag games can become very competitive — if Dave has a bad experience it may affect other activities. Try to keep the games fun and positive, without 'winners' and 'losers'.

Frozen Beanbag and Simon Says

- In Frozen Beanbag the children try to move around a play area while balancing beanbags on their heads. You can ask children to run, hop and walk backward. If the beanbag falls off, the child is 'frozen' until another child helps by picking up the beanbag and putting it back on their head. Helpers must replace the beanbag without losing their own.

- For Simon Says, one child names a body part to be moved, other children do as 'Simon Says'. Simon says 'touch your head'. Simon says 'touch your tummy and jump around'. If Simon fails to say 'Simon says' before naming a body part to be moved and a child follows the instruction, that child is out. Game continues until one child is still in and becomes the new leader.

Stephen   For Frozen Beanbag use a larger beanbag. Encourage good posture and get Stephen to visually focus on an object at head height while moving. Use different directions for moving.

Jane   Modify the rules so that the frozen children can hand the dropped beanbags to Jane, who must then put it on top of the frozen child's head.

Nicholas   Use verbal cues from others in locating dropped beanbags. Use a buddy for more dynamic movements.

Fran   Create markers for stopping and starting. Use terms that are easily understood and gestures to signal 'freeze' etc. Accompany until basic game objectives are followed independently.

Joanne   Modify rules as for Jane.

Rahul   Ensure play area is free from obstacles that children may fall over.

Dave   To reduce the competitive element of Simon Says, try a modified version that is non-elimination. This is where two games are played simultaneously. If a child is eliminated from one game they join the other. The less skilled player may switch from one game to the other but is never eliminated as such.

Eye–hand coordination

Basic equipment may be used to encourage and promote eye–hand coordination. Beanbags, balls of different shapes, sizes and textures.

Individual activities

- Hold a stick in the right hand.
- Toss it from right to left:

    Follow it from the eyes, but keep the head still.

    Bounce and catch a ball.

- Throw a beanbag into an empty ice-cream container.
- Roll a ball at a target (big to start with, then gradually made smaller).
- Throw a ball into a bucket or tin.
- Throw and catch a ball which has bounced off a wall.

Partner activities

Stand opposite a partner:

- Roll a ball for a partner to stop.
- Roll it through a partner's legs (wide to narrow).
- Bounce a ball for a partner to catch.
- Throw a beanbag into a container held in the air and to the side of partner.
- Stand beside a partner — run out to a given point, turn and complete all the above activities.

Progression ball

In pairs, stand about the same distance from a marked point such as an ice-cream container. Throw a ball (beanbag) to a partner. If the ball (beanbag) is caught, partner takes a step backward, but if the ball (beanbag) is dropped, partner takes one step forward. If the throw does not reach the partner, the thrower takes one step forward. The winner is the one who is the greatest distance form the marked point when the stop signal is given.

Stephen   Use the beanbag rather than the ball for throwing and catching. Alternatively use smaller, lighter and softer balls for catching and bouncing. It is important to use smaller rather than larger balls as the larger ones may encourage immature catching patterns (scooping rather than using hands). Remember that balls tossed directly to Stephen will be easier to catch than ones tossed to his side (particularly right side). Gradually introduce more difficult catching and throwing activities over time.

Jane   Allow adequate room for Jane to move using her wheelchair without disturbing the other members of the group. Ensure the 'stick' is short enough to be used while sitting.

Nicholas   Use brightly coloured balls or beanbags that are a contrast to the surroundings. Provide careful instruction, including physical assistance, so that Nicholas is ready to catch. Have partner wear brightly coloured bib and use an auditory cue to signal release.

Fran   Start partner activities by giving the ball, then progress slowly to tossing it. Make individual activities into partner ones where one child 'mirrors' what the other does. Do not do one activity for too long, use a roster and stick to the same sequence of activities each time.

Joanne   It is OK for Joanne to use one hand for catching activities. Angle the ball or beanbag to give Joanne different visual tracking tasks. She can take one push forward or backward for progression ball activity.

Rahul   Keep instruction short and sharp. Demonstrate activities first and have a practice.

Dave   Try using balls/bags with bells in. Rotate activities often and start with individual ones, introducing partners slowly. These are good activities for success so be mindful of setting targets that are difficult.

Hitting and kicking

Allow children to practice hitting with a bat. It is important that they discover how a ball moves in different ways, onto and away from the bat, and how to position themselves in relation to the ball so that they can hit it.

Individual and partner activities (hitting)

Exploration and free practice with various types of balls.

- Hit a ball

    into the air, using different parts of the body

    along a line with your hand

    high into the air and catch it

    for a partner to catch

- pretend to hit an imaginary ball: high, low and to each side

- with a ball and newspaper 'bat'

    hit the ball along the ground with small taps (follow the line)

    hit it a distance to a partner

    hit the ball, which has been rolled to a partner, back to them.

Circular cricket

Equipment:	One medium ball and one newspaper bat
Playing surface:	One marked large circle and one smaller circle inside it
Formation:	Batter stands in small circle, other children stand in free space within the larger circle
Instructions:	One player bowls underarm to the appointed batter, who hits anywhere within the large circle. If the ball is caught, hits the batter, or rolls outside the big circle, change the batter. Rotate the bowler and the batter until all the children have had a turn.

Individual and partner activities (kicking)

- Push or tap a ball around freely within a defined space, keeping it as close as possible to the feet. Use right then left foot.

- Step forward and kick a stationary ball.

- Run and kick a stationary ball.

- Kick a rolling ball — in different directions and over various distances.

- Kick a ball along the ground to a partner about 5 m away. Partner stops it with hands and kicks it back.

- 'Low' bounce the ball to a partner who attempts to kick it back.

- In pairs, try to make as many continuous passes as possible, without the ball stopping or going out of control.

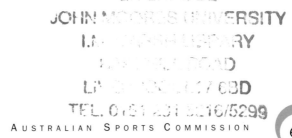

Skittle ball

Equipment: Five skittles (milk cartons, tins, blocks of wood) and one medium sized ball.

Instructions: Place skittles about 10 cm apart in a V formation. Get children to stand about 2 m from the objects and kick ball to knock them down. Each child has a turn and counts the number of skittles knocked down.

Stephen Stephen will normally kick with his left leg, using the right leg for balance. If may be that he finds it easier to run and kick rather than to kick from a stationary position. Children with spastic CP often find it easier to engage in activities that are continuous rather than broken up. Experiment to find what works best and encourage good technique (preparation and follow through).

Jane Encourage Jane to participate in kicking activities out of her wheelchair — without forcing the issue. Try modifying circular cricket so that all the children are sitting during play — a smaller playing area may be required. Make sure household obstacles are wide apart for 'dribbling' and assign a buddy for assistance if required.

Nicholas Use larger, brighter coloured balls (or balls with bells in if available), and provide good feedback relating to distance. Paint the skittles different colours and experiment to find out the preferred distance for kicking.

Fran Blow a whistle (or similar auditory cue) to signal start and stop. Make a target for all kicking activities and reward Fran for success.

Joanne It is important to encourage Joanne to use her left leg for kicking — try sitting during activities or see if Joanne can kick into the air from her wheelchair — may need to stabilise her wheelchair before starting the activity.

Rahul Brief a buddy to ensure 'heading' activities are avoided. Vary the distance between play areas if necessary. Use larger, softer, bright coloured balls.

Dave Close off Dave's area to minimise distractions. Encourage Dave to take the lead and adopt his own way of doing things.

Dribbling practice activities

Exploration and free practice with various types of balls. Try encouraging children to dribble a ball:

- along a line

- around a circle

- and stop with it under control

- in and out of a line of cones

- to pass a partner who acts as a defender

- and shoot for goal

Stephen Break the dribbling skill down into smaller parts — work on gaining control with both right and left sides at a slow pace. Stephen prefers to support on left side and kick with right for soccer, but encourage kicking with either. During any game, position Stephen as a right sided player. Try a partly deflated ball in the beginning.

Jane For soccer dribbling skills allow Jane to control the ball by turning her wheelchair side on — if the ball hits the centre of the wheel it has been controlled. A partner can retrieve the ball and give it to Jane to throw as if passing. Make a rule that opposing players can only come within a certain distance of the wheelchair.

Nicholas Use clear, distinct lines marked on the ground for reference. Use larger, softer balls if it helps and ensure obstacles are marked. Visual demonstrations should be accompanied with good auditory instruction using 'left', 'right', 'forward', 'backward' — not 'there', 'here' etc.

Fran Rotate dribbling stations in a set manner. Physically assist basic skills if necessary and model simple component parts of the skill on an individual basis while others practice.

Joanne For hockey type dribbling activities use a lighter stick and an air ball, as Joanne may have difficulties using one arm for extended periods.

Rahul The use of skill stations should help Rahul work on developing skills in a group situation where every child works at their own level.

Dave Vary activities in quick succession mixing simple activities with ones that require greater effort and skill. Introduce rewards for completion and constantly encourage good effort and performance.

2.2.3 Secondary to post-compulsory

Students are at a stage when their bodies, social behaviour and emotions are changing rapidly. They are aware of their developing sexuality. Peer group acceptance remains important, but there is a gradual increase in the importance of individual friendships. They have an increasing desire for autonomy and independence.

They challenge social control and values more frequently and question rules imposed by authority figures. They are more able to appreciate the positions, views and rights of others, and moral awareness and beliefs about social justice begin to emerge.

Below there are a number of 'traditional' individual, dual and team sports and games that are relatively easy to adapt for young people with disabilities.

Some 'disability specific' activities are also examined. Activities such as boccia and throlf are exciting and fun, and of great benefit to all young people.

ACTIVITIES

Gymnastics

General considerations

Balance beam

- Start by using a taped line on the gym floor, introducing new skills slowly.

- Change the height of the beam until it suits the individual person.

- Place mats under the beam for the spotter to stand on.

- Teach every student how to fall, that grabbing at the beam can be dangerous and that pushing away from the beam is the correct method.

Horizontal bar

- Begin by using the bar at shoulder height.

- Ensure that each student has sufficient strength (in grip, arm and shoulder) before progressing onto more difficult exercises.

Floor exercises

- Using markers on the floor will give the students guided reference points and help in the developing a sense of direction and distance.

- Make sure that static exercises are performed well before progressing onto movement activities.

- Vary the distance between moves, gradually increasing as skills develop.

- Ensure that soft areas are used and surround the activity area.

Stephen Make sure Stephen performs a thorough relaxing warm-up before the balance beam activity in particular. This will help reduce tenseness during the activity. Flexibility and strength activities are very valuable and these should be encouraged.

Jane Seek advice over whether Jane should take part in activities that may dislodge the shunt. Lower the bar for Jane but encourage the development of strength gaining exercises.

Nicholas Make sure Nicholas has been orientated to the apparatus first. With the beam attach bright pieces of cloth to the ends and have some auditory cues located directly at the end facing. Ensure all ground areas are free from obstacles and there is plenty of room to work in.

Fran Use markers and stationary cues to signify stations. Use different and repeated signals for stop, start and move on. Do not clutter the environment with unnecessary apparatus.

Joanne Allow Joanne to perform activities in wheelchair. Work on following a straight line and on manoeuvring within confined spaces. With floor exercises encourage upper body movement, style and form. If possible get other students to perform activities while seated in a wheelchair.

Rahul Seek advice before beginning any gymnastic activity with Rahul. Atlantoaxial instability may prohibit participation in rolling type activities. Devise alternative exercises such as rolls from side to side rather than forwards.

Dave Some of these exercises can be physically draining so try to mix the intensity and frequency of exercise so that Dave can have rest or down periods. Provide rewards and incentives that are easily achievable. This will help motivation in activities that do not have obvious immediate outcomes.

Track and field

General considerations

- Using buddy systems often has great benefits in track and field activities. Partnering young people with disabilities and their peers has a 'two-way' benefit as one interacts with another. Ensure that any medical and/or safety issues are clear before any activity begins.

- Change distances and introduce 'handicap' events if you feel it is necessary and if it does not affect the integrity of the activity.

- Use adapted equipment where appropriate including junior sized apparatus and soft or 'rubberised' equipment.

- Encourage young people to adopt alternative movement and postural patterns. Let them experiment and find the easiest method.

Stephen Use large grips that are soft or are rubber based. Remember to incorporate flexibility exercise before short bursts of strenuous activity.

Jane During seated throwing activities make sure the wheelchair is secure. The easiest method is for a buddy to hold tightly onto the back of the chair, with fingers well clear of the wheels, while crouching behind it. Make sure the buddy is below and behind the range of follow through for the throwing arm.

Nicholas Discuss appropriate adaptations with Nicholas. Suggest a buddy with a guide rope for longer running distances or a caller set at certain distances apart for shorter distances. Auditory cues can be used at take-off marks.

Fran If activities are carried on outdoors, choose an area with very few distractions. Mark activity areas clearly and rotate activities in a set manner.

Joanne Most track and field type activities can be done indoors or on a synthetic surface where Joanne will be able to use her wheelchair. Secure wheelchair for throwing activities as for Jane. Joanne should be able to participate in most activities by herself or with the assistance of a buddy.

Rahul Rahul should be able to take part in most activities although advice should be taken when programming activities such as high jump. Praise and reward effort and plan for success.

Dave Look at the type of auditory cues and instruction being used for different activities. Design alternatives if appropriate, such as hand signals, use of lights, notices and clearly marked boundaries and edges.

Throlf

Throlf is an activity adapted from golf suitable for all young people. It can be played indoors or outdoors and uses very simple equipment.

Equipment: 6–8 hoops, 6–8 cones, various obstacles (chairs, tables), beanbags or sponge balls.

Playing surface: Marked course of 6–8 holes (hoops), each hole far enough apart to suit the varying abilities of the students.

Instructions: Each student starts at the tee (marked by each cone) by tossing the beanbag (the ball) to land inside the hoop (the hole). If they miss, another 'shot' is taken until the beanbag lands in the hoop. Place obstacles (bunkers), such as chairs and tables, around each hoop. Each student keeps score by the number of throws it takes to complete the course.

Modified boccia

Boccia is a Paralympic sport played by people with cerebral palsy. It is a game of skill and strategy that can be modified and enjoyed by all students.

Equipment: One circle target area similar to an archery target marked on the floor; beanbags or soft balls in two colours (for two sides).

Playing surface: Indoors or outdoors, small marked circle surrounding the target.

Instructions: Students sit or kneel in a circle 2–3 m from the target area marked on the floor. Make two teams and arrange the seating so that each student is seated next to a member of the opposite team. The target area is marked like an archery target in scoring zones, the highest score being the bullseye. Each student must toss or roll the beanbag or ball as close as possible to the bullseye. As each student takes a turn they can push the opponent's marker away from the highest scoring areas. Only count the three or four highest scoring throws in the final tally.

Stephen Encourage Stephen to use both hands for throwing, with all students using beanbags.

Jane No adaptation is required for Jane.

Nicholas Use brightly coloured beanbags or balls. A buddy can explain the layout and distances of throlf courses and boccia targets. Orient Nicholas to throlf obstacles before the game begins.

Fran These are excellent activities for Fran, as courses and procedures can remain stable with set, easy to follow, rules and regulations. Allow Fran to observe others playing first and praise good shots and throws whenever appropriate.
Try designing a cue card with a picture of the activity that Fran can relate to whenever each activity is programmed.

Joanne No adaptation is required.

Rahul Explain rules as simply and clearly as possible and initially have a buddy accompany Rahul around the course. The buddy should encourage Rahul to keep his score and provide feedback with respect to correct distances, trajectories and directions.

Dave Use manual demonstration as the main form of instruction and try to begin a game as soon as possible. Keep the interest levels high with short, sharp games that are fun and not too competitive.

Basketball

Basketball is a game played by many people with disabilities. Australian has very successful wheelchair basketball teams that compete in all the major international events. In school settings, where young people with a variety of abilities are included, try some of the following variations:

- Allow the wheelchair user to replace the traditional dribble with a bounce after every two pushes (ie as used in wheelchair basketball).

- For fouls, remember that the wheelchair is part of the body.

- Perhaps have the young person in a wheelchair concentrate on offence rather than defence so chasing is kept to a minimum.

- Make a rule that able-bodied opponents cannot come within a certain distance of the wheelchair when passing and that an opponent cannot tie up a ball in the possession of the person in the wheelchair.

- For students who have a vision impairment, zonal offence and defence markers can be placed in set positions on the court to act as reference points.

- Make a bounce pass obligatory to persons with vision impairment.

- Modify rules so that all players must handle the ball during an offensive play.

- Make sure that all lines are clearly marked and all unnecessary obstacles are taken away from the side of the court.

- Less mobile players or young people using wheelchairs could play at the front of the zonal defence, blocking more effectively defensively and being ready for the fast break offensively.

Stephen Position Stephen as a left sided offensive player for games but work on right side movement and skill development during practice. Use a lighter ball with good pimpled grip. Slow the pace of competitive games, ie walking only; reinforce the non-contact rule strictly.

Jane Hire out some wheelchairs for use by all the group and contact the local wheelchair basketball association about rules, demonstrations, etc.

Nicholas Make sure all court markings are clearly drawn and rings and backboards are highlighted in some way. Make a rule that players must keep a certain distance apart during play. Place an auditory cue behind the ring for shooting practice.

Fran Reduce the size of playing teams. Mark an area to practice shooting on the wall with Fran's name. Use single auditory cues to signal actions such as 'hands up', 'block' and 'stop'.

Joanne Use same tactics as with Jane. With a buddy work out a series of quick cues to signal forward, backward, left, right, stop, start... Buddy can only react to those cues as Joanne is pushed around the court. Lower the height of the ring if appropriate.

Rahul Match Rahul with similar sized opponents. Take each skill and break it down into smaller units for practice. Make a rule that all players must handle the ball during practice and during play.

Dave Think about court position for Dave. A back court position means Dave can observe and react to things in front of him rather than relying on auditory cues from players behind.

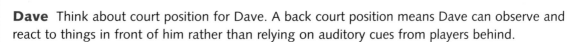

2.2.4 Young people with high support needs

For various reasons, often the physical activity needs of people with high support needs are overlooked. This could be due to a lack of resources, assistance, or equipment. It could also result from a lack of understanding of the value of physical activity to people whose physical or intellectual abilities are often very restricted within the confines of a 'regular' setting. These people do, however, have a right to the same opportunities for movement experience as any other young person and the principles of adaptation remain the same.

Functional ability

The levels of functional ability of people with high support needs vary enormously. Similarly, the level of practical assistance required also varies, although more often than not some degree of personal assistance with basic movement patterns is needed. The ability to function as independently as possible depends on many factors. Your program of activity can have profound effects on developing functional ability levels that are invaluable later in life. It might also provide one of the few genuine movement experiences available for young people who are 'trapped' by inactivity.

Benefits of activity

In addition to the usual benefits of physical activity, people with high support needs benefit from physical activity through:

- improved physiological functioning, including muscle strength and endurance
- improved motor ability, including head control and trunk balance
- improved mobility, including basic movement patterns such as crawling, rolling, walking and pushing a wheelchair
- improved motor skills such as grasping, releasing, pushing, pulling, and kicking
- improved social interaction
- reduced negative behaviour such as rocking, head banging, hand chewing
- improved ability to follow simple instructions such as stop, go, no, yes
- building up tolerance of being handled as well as the ability to assist in personal care.

Supportive environment

Your ability to influence the physical development of people with high support needs is, of course, influenced by the levels of assistance provided for during classes. It is undoubtedly a great challenge to construct an individualised physical activity program for a person with high support needs within the confines of the regular setting. But careful planning and a willingness to explore new ways of developing activities for people of very diverse abilities will go a long way towards success. It is imperative that you consult parents and medical personnel before embarking on any program. Involve parents in the initial stages. Do not leave it all up to somebody else, they may not always be available.

Progress can take a great deal of time and can be seemingly very small. Try to develop strategies that will not only motivate the person to participate but will also help motivate yourself to continue to push movement possibilities. Try some of these basic strategies:

- Make a conscious effort to enjoy the activity yourself. If you begin with a positive and fun perspective, it will invariably rub off on your child.
- Do activities with the individual — make it fun by using music and rhymes if appropriate.
- Do not expect a person to just stop inappropriate behaviour — try to replace it with positive activities.
- Make your activities colourful and change them around to add variety. Use different settings and environments and try not to restrict activities to inside the school walls!
- Use the same piece of equipment in different ways — explore new possibilities.

- Improvise and think laterally — subtle changes can make big differences, and don't reject an idea if it doesn't work the first time.

- Where possible use age-appropriate equipment and rules.

- Use user-friendly equipment such as soft toys and home made bats.

> *When working with a child with severe multiple impairments — a child with little large muscle movement — the primary goal is to get the child to move — any part in any fashion, but move! We learn how to use our bodies through actual use. Muscular capabilities only improve through activity – something must happen physically.*
>
> Gross et al (1989) 176

Three approaches for including young people with high support needs

Extending the skill stations approach

One method, which has been used successfully in both regular and special school, is a skill stations approach. The use of skill stations is nothing new. An extension of the skill stations approach should allow people with high support needs to take part in the same age-appropriate activities as their peers (Block, Provis and Nelson 1993).

Consider the format of the traditional skill station approach for dribbling a soccer ball:

SKILL STATION SET UP FOR DRIBBLING A SOCCER BALL
1. controls ball at feet while walking
2. controls ball while walking quickly
3. controls ball while jogging forward
4. controls ball while running forward
5. controls ball while weaving between cones
6. controls ball while jogging forward and weaving between cones
7. controls ball with a cross-over dribble while walking between cones
8. controls ball while running forward and weaving between cones
9. controls ball with a cross-over dribble while running forward
10. controls ball while being marked by opponent going at 3/4 pace

In this traditional station set up there may be groups of three to five people assigned to any one of the ten stages, depending on skill levels. After five to ten minutes at each station the participants may rotate and move on to the next. The stages of each station will normally cover the range of ability levels found in the regular setting. People with high support needs may begin at the lower level of the continuum.

By extending the scope of the continuum and incorporating alternative ways to accomplish similar skills, people with high support needs can be included in the activity with their peers. An extended skills station approach differs from the traditional model in that it:

- extends the continuum so that lower skill levels can be incorporated
- shortens the gap between stages so slower progress can be recorded
- provides for alternative ways in which the skill can be performed.

An extended skill station basically operates in the same way as a traditional skill station. Skills are listed hierarchically in the same way, but they begin at a lower level and have smaller increments.

Alternative ways of performing the skill are described at specific increments so that people with high support needs can work toward the same movement goals but in different ways.

For example:

Joanne may be unable to dribble a soccer ball around a set of cones in the traditional manner but may be able to move around the cones while holding onto a ball secured on a lap tray.

An extended skill station for Joanne might look like:

SKILL STATION SET UP FOR DRIBBLING A SOCCER BALL (JOANNE)
1. touches ball placed on lap
2. holds ball on lap
3. holds ball on lap while pushed slowly around gym
4. manoeuvres wheelchair to side-on position for trapping
5. completes a series of successful traps
6. completes trap and guides aid short distance
7. completes a series of successful passes by throwing to a partner
8. holds onto ball while being pushed between cones
9. holds onto ball while being pushed at 3/4 speed between cones
10. completes a series of trap, pass and dribble movements

In this way Joanne is able to practise skill development, working toward the same movement goal, with same age peers, albeit in a different manner. Each student is able to work independently on skill development, at their own level and in a way that is tailored toward their own abilities. No person has to conform to the standards of the group and learning outcomes can easily be incorporated in accord with each person's level.

Using 'recess' as a way to include

In most school settings 'recess' is a time when teachers have the opportunity to escape from their students and chat to colleagues. For students, free time can be the most fun time of the day and a time when friendships are formed and cliques developed. Free play time can also be the most alienating time of the day for young people with high support needs. Individual differences can be heightened as *ad hoc* games and activities take place on more traditional formats.

Although planning recess activities seems contrary to the purpose of free play and perhaps beyond the scope of teacher responsibilities some thoughtful recess 'facilitating' can benefit all, not least those young people who are isolated because of their different abilities. Facilitating playground activities gives young people the opportunity to make choices and take part in a manner they feel is appropriate. They can come and go as they please and change activities to suit their needs. Recess time is a time when attitudes and stereotypes can be attacked head-on and the full benefits of inclusion can be seen.

Passentino and Cranfield (1994) have developed a number of guidelines for beginning a recess program. They point out that selecting recess activities is complicated by the nature of recess itself as an unstructured period of free play. When planning recess activities, keep these guidelines in mind:

- make activities accessible to all students
- use activities that have few rules and regulations
- make fun the basis of selecting activities — they should attract participants
- select activities that allow students the freedom to come and go as they please
- allow any number of participants to take part
- use age-appropriate activities, and
- suggest rather than tell, facilitate rather than instruct.

Try to build up a repertoire of activities that you can work on to improve. Suggest ideas that are working to other members of staff involved in playground duty. Some other useful hints on making recess activities inclusive are:

- have safe equipment (eg hoops, frisbees) available for use
- encourage the development of appropriate social skills among the group (eg teaching or assisting high fives for young people with high support needs)
- use modern music with a good beat
- make the atmosphere more informal than would usually be the case (use first names or nicknames)
- talk about disabilities if asked, focusing on ability and similarities rather than differences
- where appropriate, intervene and facilitate interactions between students with and without disabilities
- praise and encourage all students to take part.

Using recess as a time to encourage friendships and interaction among young people with high support needs and their peers is an excellent way to help young people learn about individual differences. Friendships in the playground will be friendships in the class. The success of inclusion may hinge on a moment or two of real positive interaction that you can encourage during recess.

Focusing on student potential

When working with students with high support needs, work from a potential theory rather than a deficit theory. This means focusing on what the student can achieve rather than what they cannot do. The following approach might help the teacher to maximise outcomes for students with high support needs:

- begin activities with a statement of current functioning
- address goals/objectives/outcomes according to this statement

- match activities with the goals of an individual education plan wherever possible
- develop appropriate strategies/resources
- evaluate according to outcomes using the statement.

Ask the following questions:

Statement of current functioning	What are his/her present skills?
Short and long-term goals	Where do we want them to be?
Strategies/resources	How do we get there?
Evaluation	How do we know when we've arrived?

Use the team approach to programming. Share your goals and activities with therapists/teaching staff/parents and encourage other team members to contribute to targeted skill development in their settings (transfer of training).

2.2.5 Young people with degenerative conditions

Students who have degenerative conditions (eg muscular dystrophy, cystic fibrosis) might be less able to participate fully in the program as activities become more physically challenging and their condition deteriorates. The degenerative effects can be fast or slow, or the student's condition might at times appear quite stable. As the student's condition progresses, it does not mean that they will be unable to participate in the activity program. Over time you will need to look at different ways of participating.

Remember:

- Do not underestimate the value of being physically active for the maintenance of each individual's health and well-being

- Encourage students to maximise their current abilities. Don't compare current functioning with previous abilities

- Work with other support personnel such as physiotherapists to ensure physical activity programs support the goals of their current therapy program and vice versa

- Try to develop skills that the student can participate in later in life, eg boccia - a game that can be easily played with limited muscle involvement

- Look for other ways for students to become more involved, even though they might be less physically active. Involvement in such programs as the Sport Education and Physical Education Program can increase as physical abilities decrease. In addition, this program should be an option not just for students with disabilities — there are benefits for all students.

The Sport Education and Physical Education Program was developed by the Australian Sports Commission in 1995. It enables all participants not only to participate, but also to take on roles (which can be rotated) in officiating, coaching and other support positions. It is a very useful extension to basic physical activity, enabling all participants to explore the game more fully and to develop their own interests and skills in relation to sport and physical activity.

Section 3
Opening doors for people with disabilities

Contents

3.1 Introduction   **79**

    3.1.1   Links between schools and clubs   80

    3.1.2   Establishing closer relationships with schools   80

3.2 What's behind the door?   **83**

    3.2.1   Why include people with disabilities?   83

    3.2.2   What's in it for me — the individual   83

    3.2.3   What's in it for me — the organisation   83

    3.2.4   Other things to consider   87

3.3 Is your door open?   **90**

    3.3.1   What is accessibility?   90

    3.3.2   The audit   93

3.4 Locksmith's report   **94**

    3.4.1   Developing an audit   94

    3.4.2   Attitudes of club members   96

    3.4.3   Orientation   97

    3.4.4   Fitting in   97

    3.4.5   Physical accessibility   98

3.5 Impressive doorknobs, shiny keys   **100**

    3.5.1   Target groups   100

    3.5.2   Develop your product   101

    3.5.3   Reach out   101

'Change what you can change, accept what you can't change, and have the ability to recognise the difference'

Annabel Bishop

Participation, according to several definitions, is about taking part or sharing with others in activities. If that is the case, I could say that I have participated in many different activities throughout my life from leisure-based activity to competitive sport activity.

During my childhood, I consider that playing was a significant contribution toward development of skills, which led to active participation in sports and recreation. It meant that I took part in a diversity of fun activities with my brothers and other children before taking part in organised sports.

My competitive and determined character may be traced back to childhood play activities with my brothers and other children. I would do daring things such as swinging as high as I could, picking up a mean-looking lizard to scare people and proving that I could do this or that.

Throughout my childhood and teenage years, I participated in numerous organised sports such as gymnastics, tennis, netball, swimming, water polo and surf lifesaving. All of these were purely for enjoyment, social interaction and also to give me the buzz of learning something new each week.

I loved participating in PE at school. I recall the day the PE teacher in primary school asked me to play netball for the school (I was in Grade 4 and the team was Grade 6 girls) and I had never heard of nor played netball before in my life. I played without any problems. Another PE teacher in secondary school was surprised to see the other side of me when I showed my 'strong determined' character while playing basketball as PE activity. I wanted to show the boys that I could play their kind and style of game!

Swimming was a sport where I excelled. I swam in mainstream (or able-bodied) competitions including state and national championships. It was an extraordinary experience for me to participate in an elite level of competitive swimming because I did not have strong aspirations to be an 'elite' swimmer of national/international calibre. All I was interested in was to swim and enjoy the moments as they came. It gave me opportunities to travel, compete in different environment, and meet new people, learning new skills and so forth.

At this point, you may wonder what disability I have. I have profound hearing loss in both ears as a result of my mother contracting rubella (German measles) during her pregnancy.

On the international level, I participated in three World Deaf Games (1981, 1985, and 1989) where I rewarded myself with a handful of medals. I found the experience life enriching and it showed me what

I am capable of doing in life. The World Deaf Games are similar to the Olympic Games or Paralympic Games but cater only for people who are deaf (criteria is an average hearing loss of 55 decibels or more).

I graduated with a Bachelor of Applied Science (Recreation Planning and Management) from the University of South Australia in 1996. A combination of my sporting background and university degree enables me to be involved in supporting and educating people with disabilities. Whenever I can, if time permits, I assist and participate in the delivery of workshops such as 'Willing and Able' and 'Coaching Athletes with Disabilities' courses.

To sum it up, I would encourage people to participate in activities whether these are leisure-based, recreational, or competitive, that suit their interests, enjoyment, and capabilities.

3.1 Introduction

In section 2 we looked at inclusion within the school setting. But what happens when school is finished? At school, young people with disabilities often have good support networks and structures set up to facilitate inclusion. When the young person finishes school, where does he or she go? This is an issue for all young people who want to continue in sport, but it is particularly relevant for people with disabilities.

This section highlights the advantages of marketing clubs to people with a disability as a means of attracting them to become active and valued club members. The section will help clubs who want to develop marketing programs, and explores in detail how they might go about doing this. Although many sporting examples are used, the basic principles of marketing remain the same whether it is an outdoor club, a community centre, an interest group, hobby or leisure club that wants to grow.

In this section we will consider how and why clubs might choose to include people with disabilities in their organisations. We discuss the benefits of being an organisation that encourages participation of people with a disability, and we explore strategies and planning processes to assist management committees.

Throughout this module we will use the door as a metaphor. By using the symbol of the door to represent an organisation we can visualise two different outcomes: a door can be either open and welcoming, or used as a barrier to keep out unwanted visitors. The people behind the door choose how they greet those on the outside.

The following elements are important in helping organisations that wish to include people with disabilities:

- identifying the value of involving people with a disability

- determining the accessibility of an organisation

- identifying areas of possible change

- developing strategies that allow for change

- reviewing possible marketing initiatives

- identifying sources of assistance

Active Australia has a commitment to help clubs and organisations address these issues through what is known as the *Provider Process*. The Provider Process acknowledges and builds on the fact that your club or organisation also has a commitment to improving its delivery of sport and physical activity for people with disabilities.

The Provider checklist is a tool that enables your club or organisation to review and improve your current operations in seven key areas: leadership, planning, information, human resources, client focus, quality of service and overall performance. Throughout this section we will refer to elements of the Provider checklist. For more detail on the Provider Process contact **1300 130 121**.

3.1.1 Links between schools and clubs

Section 2 highlighted ways that schools could help students with disabilities join in physical activities. It was stressed that there was little or no difference when planning activities for students with disabilities compared to other students and that teachers simply continued with 'best practice' teaching strategies.

There are many ways that clubs and schools can work together to their mutual benefit. Sharing equipment, resources, expertise, personnel and facilities has many advantages for both schools and clubs, which can lead to younger people and their families becoming members of your club.

3.1.2 Establishing closer relationships with schools

The 'How to' guide...

Survey current members to find out which schools they have links with

There may be students, parents or members of your club who can assist with introductions to local schools.

Decide what your club could offer

Make sure you start small and can deliver what you offer. You may like to offer one or more of the following:

- information about a 'sign-up' day
- information about your club
- loans of equipment
- use of grounds and/or pavilion
- assistance of officials
- first aid or fitness advice
- coaching
- tournament details for local schools

Select a local school for contact

It is very important to telephone the school to check the name of the contact and get a fax number. The person may be the sports or Physical Education coordinator. In schools without sports teachers, a grade teacher may be in charge of sporting activities.

- Phone the person to introduce yourself and the club. Make an offer. Explain how they can contact you to discuss the offer further. Fax the information you have discussed and further details.
- If you cannot phone or fax, you should write personally to the contact.
- Arrange to meet the contact and discuss whether they are interested in your offer. Ask if they are in a school sports district, and ask for the secretary's name. Decide when the agreed activity will take place.
- Arrange a planning meeting, if necessary.

The planning session

Make sure these details are covered:

- what the activity will be

- names and contact details of people involved

- venue for the activity

- date, time, number/s and length of activity

- equipment needed and who is to supply it

- age, sex, specific sport experience of students

- ratio of students to staff

- behavioural expectations

- arrangements for unsuitable weather conditions

- any special organisational requirements of the school

- follow-up procedure

A word from a club official

'Many sports have identified the potential that people with disabilities offer as participants, officials and administrators.'

Our characters will also highlight ways that clubs and community leaders can assist individuals with disabilities to join them in physical activity.

Let's meet our characters again. They have now grown up into teenagers and young adults. They have the same range of fears, hopes, dreams and interests as any group of young people of similar ages.

Stephen	Stephen has been actively involved in the Scouting Movement since the age of seven. He initially joined scouts because his brother was involved. (Stephen's brother does not have cerebral palsy). Stephen is now a Rover and helps with Scouts every Wednesday night. Stephen's involvement has had a huge impact on his life as he has made friends, grown in confidence and learnt valuable life skills.
Jane	Jane has grown into a very confident vivacious young lady, thanks mainly to the efforts of her PE teacher. Jane began to play wheelchair basketball three years ago. She has blossomed since then. Now in her final year at high school, she is hoping to turn her love of sport into a career by studying sports management at university. Jane has spina bifida.

Nicholas	Nicholas's parents have always encouraged him to run. As both his mother and father were accomplished athletes in their own right, it is a natural progression that Nicholas would also be an elite athlete. He has represented Australia at many international competitions, including the Paralympics. Nicholas also trains, competes and is actively involved with his local athletics club. He uses a guide runner chosen from the many good runners at his club. His club is a tremendous support to Nicholas particularly at times of international competition. Nicholas's vision impairment has never been an issue to the club.
Joanne	Joanne's advanced communication skills and her 'never give up' attitude are an asset to her judo club. Whilst Joanne does not compete, due to injuries after a car accident many years ago, she still maintains a very good level of fitness through training. She has increased the fundraising and sponsorship of the club by 150% since she has taken it over.
Fran	Fran leads an active life. She works at the local factory and is involved in the local golf club. Her attention to detail is well regarded around the club and she is a valued contributor. The fact that she has autism is not an issue for the rest of the club.
Dave	Dave is seen as a role model in his community as he has really found his niche in actively promoting, organising and coaching the local football and netball youth competitions. Dave manages his diabetes through the exercise he gets while involved in the competition, which is often played over two or three days when a remote community travels to another community to play football and netball. Although the facilities are not very good, Dave is fabulous at either scrounging equipment or making do with what he has. It never seems to worry the participants anyway!
Rahul	Rahul is still the same cheerful young person that he was when he attended primary school. Although Rahul attends school in a special setting, he has many friends at his local tennis club who do not have disabilities. His attitude to life makes him one of the most liked club members. Currently Rahul represents his club in a competition for people with an intellectual disability, although he trains with other able-bodied members of the club.

3.2   What's behind the door?

Identifying why an organisation might actively encourage people with a disability to become involved with their activities

3.2.1 Why include people with disabilities?

Why would an organisation choose to make the decision to actively encourage people with a disability to become involved in their programs? Will there be anything behind the door that's worthwhile for a person with a disability? By opening the door, will the organisation gain anything that is to their benefit?

This section does not shy away from the fact that for organisations to include people with disabilities there needs to be something in it for them. It does, however, offer suggestions and strategies that may encourage management committees and existing members to look favourably on the advantages to be gained by inviting people with a disability to become members of their organisation.

3.2.2 What's in it for me — the individual

Just as individuals come to organisations with different expectations, motives and needs, the aims and missions of different organisations vary widely. It is important to understand that the WIFM (What's in it for me?) might be as varied for different organisations as it is for different individuals. This may mean that while individuals may need to choose an organisation that meets their needs carefully, so must an organisation be clear about its purpose in attracting people with a disability. Organisations need to be aware of this and have processes in place which seek to identify the needs of new members

Our characters illustrate that there is a diverse range of reasons motivating people with disabilities to join a club or organisation.

- Stephen joined Scouts because his brother joined, and now he is a Rover.

- Jane plays wheelchair basketball because she looks up to both able-bodied and wheelchair basketball players. She has a picture of Michael Jordan in her bedroom alongside an autograph from Donna Ritchie.

- Nicholas runs because his parents have encouraged him and he loves the sport.

- Joanne wants to get fit.

- Fran wants to play the sport she loves — golf.

- Dave needs to participate for health reasons.

- Rahul likes to be in a friendly environment.

3.2.3 What's in it for me — the organisation

There are many real benefits for organisations in encouraging people with a disability to join them. Organisations need to realise that people with a disability are a viable market sector worth pursuing. This section explores some of those benefits.

Benefits to the organisation may include:

- financial benefits as extra money comes from new members
- social benefits
- reinvigoration of a club with 'new blood'
- a new pool of volunteers
- a new level of elite competition
- expertise in assistance in officiating, coaching and/or administration

Organisations may also find that by improving access for people with a disability they may inadvertently encourage other groups to join, such as older adults, parents with small children or non-English speaking adults. For example the provision of ramps for people using a wheelchair may also assist mothers with prams or people recovering from injuries.

Addressing physical access issues such as clearer signage might make it easier for everyone using the organisation's building. An attitudinal change within the existing membership of the club may be seen as 'people-friendly' and membership may increase as others join a welcoming club.

It is important that the club gets 'client focused' when it comes to people with disabilities. Know who your potential clients are and what their needs and expectations are, so that products and services can be designed to meet them. Using the 'client focus' element of the Active Australia Provider process the following simple template can identify these important elements.

Try to rate your club or organisation in the following criteria, using this scale of one to five for each of the criteria:

1. have not considered
2. thinking about it *(the club or organisation has identified that it needs to address this issue and you are deciding how to approach it)*
3. starting to develop *(you are beginning to develop this element within the club or organisation and preparing to introduce it where appropriate)*
4. implementing *(you are now beginning to implement it across the club or organisation)*
5. achieving and monitoring *(you have this element in place and are actively achieving it across the club or organisation)*

Table 7: Sample client focus checklist

Client focus	1	2	3	4	5	Evidence/action	Date achieved
1. We know who our clients are.		X				Club membership list does not indicate which clients have a disability. But we have considered ways to incorporate this in future.	
2. We gather information about our clients' needs and expectations.		X				Idea that once membership form incorporates disability, a separate contact be made about their specific needs etc.	
3. We design our activities, products and services to satisfy those needs and expectations without sacrificing financial viability.			X			Some of our coaches have recruited athletes with disabilities and work with them on an individual basis. They have adapted various programs to suit.	
4. We regularly review our performance in meeting client needs and expectations.			X			In coaches' meetings the issue of disability is talked about. Needs to develop further in more formal way.	

1 Have not considered 2 Thinking about it 3 Starting to develop 4 Implementing 5 Achieving and monitoring

By going through this simple process with your club or organisation you can identify areas for improvement and hence work toward meeting the needs and expectations of people with disabilities. Appendix 10 has a blank proforma.

Extra volunteers

As noted earlier, many sports clubs face a declining membership, for a number of reasons. People are working longer hours, they have limited time to spend with their families, and more responsibility is placed on them than ever before. New members full of enthusiasm and vigour can replenish your club's volunteer stocks with renewed skills and vision.

A word from a club administrator

'Initially we could not imagine how we could include Anthony at our club, and we could not see how he could be of benefit to the club. How wrong could we be!!! Anthony is the first there on Saturday, putting most of the mats out and getting the club ready for the Saturday competition. He is also the first to volunteer for the many jobs around the club. It is hard to imagine how we managed without him.'

Social benefits

Friendships can and will develop between existing members and new members with disabilities as people begin to see **abilities** rather than disabilities. Prejudices may disappear as existing members begin to see the person with a disability as an individual.

This will have a 'feel good' value for other members, which often influences and improves morale within the organisation. Members may see that they are also valued for who they are rather than what they are and discover that their individual capabilities are recognised and celebrated.

Reinvigorate a club

Organisations are always looking for people with drive, determination and enthusiasm. People with a disability have often overcome significant obstacles in their desire to participate. They have been motivated and persistent enough to learn which keys unlock the doors that have been closed to them. Therefore they are generally *can do* people who can pass on that enthusiasm to others. Their value to the club may be that they bring to the club experience, enthusiasm and skills, which could assist and inspire others to emulate their performances. Often the introduction of such new blood can refocus other members of an organisation to re-evaluate their commitment and energy.

Access to another level of elite participants

For people who wish to participate in a sporting club there are a number of levels of participation: local, state, national, international and Paralympic/Olympic. As in all organisations, some sports people choose to play socially and not at a competitive level, while other participants will aspire to an elite level. In the disability field most sports have state competitions leading to international or Paralympic competition.

Some people with a disability can often compete in both competitions for people with a disability and able-bodied events. As a consequence, some clubs may find that some elite athletes with a disability may wish to join at a local level, not only to be part of their local community but to access a different standard of competition.

These elite athletes may be valued for their coaching potential and expert knowledge. This is a bonus organisations need to appreciate. Often when able-bodied athletes reach an elite level they leave their local club, whereas Paralympians have more opportunity to stay at their local club.

The benefits to organisations of having the expertise of elite competitors at a club are many:

- opportunities for publicity
- motivation of other members
- opportunities for coaches to be involved with elite level athletes
- development of coaches
- attraction of sponsors
- provision of role models

Financial benefits

It is important for organisations to realise that people with a disability are often working or have other sources of disposable income. Most people with a disability are able to make a financial contribution comparable to other members. They are able to pay membership fees, attend social functions and support fundraising events. For an organisation they are another potential and vital source of income.

Organisations that include people with disabilities are viewed favourably by both the local and wider community. Councils, sponsors, government agencies, and peak bodies all have an interest in encouraging access for people with disabilities. Grants are often available to assist with new programs, training of coaches or personnel and redevelopment of facilities.

3.2.4 Other things to consider

Moral and legal obligations

Sporting clubs not only have a moral obligation, they have a legal one. Anti-discrimination and equal opportunity legislation places legal obligations on organisations to provide access to people with a disability. Access does not simply mean that there are toilets and ramps appropriately placed. Access means that the organisation is actively developing and implementing strategies that will allow people with a disability to participate and become an active member of the club.

Medical and safety considerations

There are very few medical considerations that preclude a person with a disability from an activity. All organisations should request each new member to fill out a medical form and keep the records on file for safety reasons. Be aware that clubs and associations can only ask a person with a disability to complete a medical form if they do so with all members of their club. If in doubt about the suitability of an activity, simply inform the person with a disability about the skills required and the potential risks and let them decide about their suitability to compete.

Dusty's involvement in the Kewsy Athletics Club has added a new sense of excitement and purpose to the club. As a well-known Paralympian (and 400m runner) Dusty has given his club mates a new focus and the club a new direction. Whilst his profile, and constant articles in the local newspaper, give the club much needed publicity and credibility, the club supports Dusty and regularly holds functions to coincide with a major international competition Dusty is competing in. When Dusty can spare some time, he works with the club's juniors and enjoys taking an active role in their development.

Athletes with disabilities can add new dimensions to your club, as our characters below illustrate:

- **Stephen's** big family is involved in their son's Rover club. His father is support group secretary, his mother assists with the fundraising, and his older brother is the leader of the Joey Scouts. His larger extended family regularly attends functions.

- **Jane's** enthusiasm is invaluable around the club. She gives lots of her own time to assist in club duties, particularly when it involves helping the junior members of the club. She actively recruits more members, who find her enthusiasm for her sport infectious.

- **Nicholas's** profile and incredible skill level against able-bodied competitors make him an invaluable asset to the club.

- **Joanne's** determination is an asset to the club and her special skills in marketing and promotion have seen the club's sponsors grow by 150% since she has taken over the role of fundraising and sponsorship.

- **Fran** takes her job at the club very seriously. Her excellent attention to detail ensures that she always has the clubs and other equipment in perfect order. Because other club members see this important job as tedious, her input is valued and appreciated.

- **Dave's** involvement and love for sport has meant that he is a role model for all in his community. It seems that it is impossible to ignore the positive effect that activity has on Dave's life, and there is little doubt that many more people from his community are participating in activity because they see Dave's achievements.

- **Rahul's** fabulous attitude to life has an effect on other club members.

There are as many benefits for an organisation in encouraging people with a disability to join them as there are for the person. Knowing what's behind the door is one thing but deciding whether to open it is another. Organisations may need to decide why they want people with disabilities to join their club. Is it enthusiasm, elite coaching, money, new blood or diversity? Only the club can answer these questions and make the decision to actively choose to recruit members with a disability.

'Kelli's influence on the club has been profound. Her determination and skill have provided a new enthusiasm for our runners. Our results have never been better!'

'Jean has taken on many roles within our club. Before she joined us we struggled to get volunteers to assist with things like fundraising and marketing. Since she has taken over, we all have a renewed enthusiasm, and more cash!'

'We have learned many things from Dale and appreciate his valuable input into our organisation. Above all he has taught us all to look beyond our preconceptions and never to judge a book by its cover. As a result we are re-looking at everything we do and the club just has a different feel about it.'

3.3   Is your door open?

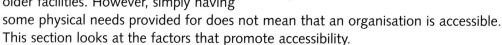

A critical look at the accessibility of organisations

Many officials and club members believe that for an organisation to be accessible to people with disabilities all that is needed is the provision of ramps, parking and toilets. Management committees are often supportive of these changes to facilities while councils and community groups make provision in their planning for new structures or redevelopment of older facilities. However, simply having some physical needs provided for does not mean that an organisation is accessible. This section looks at the factors that promote accessibility.

3.3.1 What is accessibility?

There is little value in having ramps, accessible parking and accessible toilets that allow people with a disability to gain physical access to your organisation if once they're through the door no one speaks to them or makes them feel welcome.

For example, access can be as simple as:

- knowing where the toilets are

- changing the noticeboard so that it is less cluttered and important memos are easily read

- valuing a person for their contribution

- having a 'support' person or buddy to help someone understand the way the organisation works

However, all of these access issues are important for all new members and not just those with a disability. Changing the noticeboard may help someone who wears glasses as well as one who has a vision impairment, while having a support person may be as necessary for someone who lacks confidence as someone with a disability who is new.

Most people with a disability will find a way to get in if they feel welcome. In many instances they will work around 'annoying' access problems such as a step into the clubrooms if the club is a friendly supportive one. Most people with a disability need few or no modifications to physical access. It is of more importance to ensure that existing member attitudes are receptive and inviting before allocating resources on physical items that may never be used.

All existing members of an organisation need to feel welcome within the organisation. They need to feel valued for their skills and contributions as well as being respected for who they are. New members, whether they have a disability or not, have the same needs.

Feeling welcome

Organisations can redesign their buildings to add expensive ramps, parking facilities and other amenities. But people with a disability might still not join their organisation after making initial enquiries, or might remain for only a short time.

There is no value in having ramps when there is no 'welcome mat' laid out when the person arrives. Having a designated 'welcomer' for new members, producing information packs, encouraging a supportive and warm environment or instigating a 'buddy program' where the individual works side-by-side with an established member are a few ways that organisations can make their new members feel comfortable. Recruiting drives need to have a general feeling that new members are wanted, that the organisation is not a closed shop and that all are welcome not just those specifically targeted.

There may need to be modifications to this process to accommodate the needs of specific individuals. As an example, a welcome official may need to spend more time giving auditory information to a person with vision impairment instead of relying on a printed information pack.

The Active Australia Provider checklist can be used to help identify your club or organisation's human resource needs in creating a welcoming environment for people with disabilities. Take a look at the sample checklist below and apply it to your club or organisation (see Appendix 9).

Table 8: Sample human resource checklist

Human resources	1	2	3	4	5	Evidence/action	Date achieved
1. There is a friendly and welcoming atmosphere in our club or organisation.				X		Reception staff have received training in disability awareness. Information pack done. Special offers for new members.	
2. We plan our people needs, including what skills and/or qualifications we require and what training may be needed.			X			Reception staff have attended 'Willing and Able' course. Other staff need to attend. Staff orientation needs information on disability types etc.	
3. We have policies and practices that encourage access and equity.		X				Club committee have started to consider a disability policy and Action Plan.	
4. We have enough people with skills or qualifications to carry out all necessary tasks.			X			Yes, but need to expand.	

1 Have not considered   2 Thinking about it   3 Starting to develop   4 Implementing   5 Achieving and monitoring

Feeling wanted

To be seen as a charity case is demeaning both to the individual and to the rest of the membership. It signals to the community that here is an organisation that does not accept difference or acknowledge ability, and is unconcerned with the needs of each member. It may be necessary to instigate some form of education process beginning at management level if there is a perceived lack of support. A Disability Education Program course could be useful.

See Appendix 1 for contact details of State Disability Education Program coordinators.

Education of members: how to greet and meet a member with a disability

How do you talk to a person with a disability? The same way you would speak to any person — with respect and in an open and welcoming manner. Some members may never have met a person with a disability. Many of them may have friends and relatives who have a disability but still be unsure about what is acceptable behaviour. Others may have little experience and may be unsure of how to treat a person with a disability.

The following suggestions highlight that common sense and simple courtesy remain the best approach to forming relationships.

- Offer your help when you think it might be needed but respect the individual's right to refuse assistance.

- Respect the individual's space.

- Treat equipment such as wheelchairs as part of the person — do not remove, touch or play with wheelchairs.

- Realise that people with disabilities may have different ways of doing things, that look awkward and difficult. More often than not, the individual has worked out the best way of doing something for him/herself.

- Keep the person in perspective! An arm is not the whole person.

- Recognise that people with physical disabilities are not necessarily hard of hearing and don't necessarily have an intellectual disability. There's no need to speak slower or raise your voice!

- When someone with a disability enters your club, speak to them, not their partner or friend.

- Understand that there is no such thing as a typical disability. No two people have exactly the same disability.

- Relax! Have fun! People with disabilities have the same feelings, dreams and goals as you do.

A story from Robyn

I joined a gym with my friend Judi, who is an amputee. Both of us were somewhat intimidated by the gym, our first venture into getting fit for a long time. The manager gently assured Judi that an individual program could be worked out for her and that there were many machines not requiring two arms. However, all sensitivity flew out the window as we walked across the crowded gym with the trainer. Suddenly, the manager yelled, 'Hussein, she's only got one arm — make sure you make adjustments for that'. Judi turned to me and said, 'Lucky she told him — I'm sure he wouldn't have noticed!' We joined another gym.

In many instances able-bodied members may feel awkward in talking to or involving people with a disability. It may be necessary to have some form of orientation or education workshop for existing members to make them feel at ease when interacting with new members who may have a disability.

Contributing to the organisation

People with a disability, as any other members, need to feel as if they are contributing in some way to their organisation. This contribution could be financial, through their successes in competition, their coaching skills or their administrative expertise.

Making sure all voices are heard

It is also extremely important that their opinions are considered and given the same weight as any other member of the organisations. To maintain the morale of the organisation, members must be seen to be equal and individuals not rated differently. All members need to feel a sense of ownership of the organisation and feel that they are contributors.

Good access is:

* **good citizenship**
* **good business**
* **good for everyone**

3.3.2 The audit

How do organisations find out if they are accessible? Conducting an audit of the accessibility of your organisation is the first step to opening your door. Organisations may feel comfortable addressing the physical issues — such as provision of ramp access, or products such as welcome /information booklets — but they might experience difficulties when assessing attitudes within the club. The audit process *does not* have to be expensive or long and complex.

In order to open the door of your organisation it needs to be accessible. Accessibility is not just about ramps and accessible toilets but more importantly about being welcoming and valuing the contributions a person with a disability can bring to the organisation. Audits help achieve understanding of how accessible an organisation is and need not be overly complicated. For any organisation audits have the added benefit of improving facilities and access for *everyone*.

3.4 Locksmith's report

3.4.1 Developing an audit

The key to opening the door is to know exactly what kind of lock it is. Without basic understanding of what is happening within an organisation, what resources are available and what attitudes members have, any marketing strategy will not work. Committing time and energy to good pre-planning will contribute greatly to the success of any marketing initiative. Knowing how and why an organisation works, listening to key players and assessing 'hidden messages' are all important.

The first step in any planning must be the organisation audit. The more information and pre-planning that is done, the better prepared the organisation is, the better the chance of success.

A sample audit form may look like this (see also Appendix 10):

Table 9: Sample audit sheet

Accessibility	Yes/no	Brainstorm solutions
• **Location** *How can new members access your club? Is the club close to transport?*		
• **Parking/drop-off** *Do members or drivers need accessible parking?Are the car parks located close to entrances? Is the surface of the par park suitable for people with mobility difficulties? Is there a procedure to ensure that people are safe on arrival or departure?*		*Witches hats out* *Submission to council for spaces*
• **Welcome procedure** *Tour of facility. How are members welcomed? How are they supported in their introduction to the club? Is there a check to ensure that they have settled in?*		*Train some members* *Ask Mary and Phil — they're great at making people feel welcome!*
• **Signage** *Do signs indicate important features. (eg reception, toilets, canteen, exit)? Are they clearly written and visible? Are universal symbols used?*		*Use Pete's contact with signwriter approx. cost $50*
• **Ramps/pathways** *Is there a clear, safe pathway joining all main features? Are all areas easily accessed by people with mobility difficulties?*		*Bob sets up two planks and a board at 9am for Joanne Ramp submission to council*
• **Toilets** *Are toilets located for quick access?Are they suitable for mobility difficulties? Is privacy assured for all people?*		*Contact council about funding* *Consult Nicholas's uncle (who uses a wheelchair) to see if there are simple measures we can take to make the toilets more accessible*
• **Activity environments** *Is the facility safe and clear of clutter? Can people move about independently? Is the area adequately lit, and cooled or heated?*		
• **Resources (human, physical and financial)** *Does the club have the necessary equipment to support inclusion? Are additional support staff required?* *(continued next page)*		

Table 9: Sample audit sheet (continued)		
Accessibility	**Yes/no**	**Brainstorm solutions**
Policies and procedures: Are there provisions for addressing people with disabilities? Is there a grievance procedure to address issues? Is there a procedure to ensure activity staff are aware of medical issues? *Training and information: Do coaches or other staff need additional training? Do other members of the club need additional training? Are members/coaches and other staff supportive of people with disabilities?*		

The audit needs to examine in detail:

- attitudes of the management committee
- attitudes of the existing membership
- attitudes of key players in the organisation
- orientation procedures
- whether new members are 'fitting in'
- physical access

The audit sheet may include a questionnaire to members about their attitudes to and concerns about people with a disability. It should combine elements of all the key points for a balanced view of what is happening within the organisation. Importantly, what an audit should not do is rely solely on the physical access elements and ignore the hidden elements within a club.

There are four main issues that need to be addressed within the audit process. Management committees will need to closely examine the audit to establish where their members and the club stand on these issues, and act to address them if necessary. How the organisation chooses to obtain this information will be discussed in this section but the organisation should concentrate efforts on gathering information on attitudes of club membership, orientation procedures, 'unwritten' information and physical access.

3.4.2 Attitudes of club members

Attitude is everything! Sometimes the general membership or specific individuals have fears and preconceptions about people with disabilities. Some negative feelings may emanate from their lack of experience or contact with people with a disability or past segregation practices within the community. Often, initial negative feelings change when individuals become known as people and as valuable contributing members.

If negative feelings can be identified then members may become aware of prejudices and act positively to change attitudes. Attitudes are not set in concrete! However, if the general membership of the organisation is unwilling to accept people with a disability or their access relies on a key person, then it is unlikely that it will ever be truly accessible. If negative attitudes prevail towards people with a disability then it is likely that these attitudes exist to other groups in the community such as older/younger people, Indigenous populations, and people from a non English speaking background.

For this reason one of the primary objectives may be to educate the membership about people with a disability. This might involve conducting a disability awareness course such as a 'Willing and Able' course or a CAD ('Coaching Athletes with Disabilities') course, depending on the needs of your sporting, leisure or recreational club. An alternative is that an individual with a disability may address the members. It may be appropriate to conduct a demonstration event or a 'come and try' day.

In most instances, the first person joining an organisation paves the way for others. It therefore helps if the initial attempt is by a committed person willing to accept that there may be some early resistance from some members.

3.4.3 Orientation

For the benefit of *all* new members the orientation process should be well prepared so that the new member feels comfortable as quickly as possible. Any new member needs some orientation in a new environment. However, not all people with a disability will need special treatment or modified orientation processes.

Orientation could take the form of an information package outlining rules and regulations, with details of uniform, names of committee members, and contact phones numbers. It might also cover:

* introduction to key members

* introduction to a supportive 'buddy' with responsibility for the initial joining stage

* tour of facilities

* explanation of codes of conduct

* allocation of parking space/locker

* safety and emergency procedures

Depending on the type of disability a person has, the information package may need to be modified. For example, if the member has a vision impairment, a taped information package may be required or information may need to be repeated so that the new member is able to revisit information until it is clear and easily remembered.

If a 'welcomer' believes that a person needs extra support, the best step is just to ask them. Most people with a disability will know when to ask for extra help.

3.4.4 Fitting in

In most organisations there are unwritten laws, informal lines of communication and acceptable behaviour practices. These need to be identified and explained.

Sometimes a new member with a disability may not have a finely tuned understanding of the subtle differences between acceptable and unacceptable behaviour in your club, particularly if they are new to your type of organisation. Perhaps assigning them a 'buddy', who can show them the ropes and assist with the orientation process, is a good idea.

3.4.5 Physical accessibility

Costly and time-consuming modifications will be largely unnecessary but minor changes might need to be made. The audit process may uncover problems that will not only make it easier for the person with a disability but will also make access easier for the general membership.

Some example of minor modifications are:

* installing some type of ramp or handrail
    will also assist less mobile members
    will also prevent slipping when ramp is wet

* putting padding on sharp edges
    has a safety benefit for members, and for small children of members

The most important result of any audit is that once specific issues are identified these can be corrected before the marketing plan is instigated. Consequently, organisations need to spend time evaluating what is happening in their organisation, decide what needs fixing, celebrate what is working and decide where they want to go before they can achieve anything.

Just because an organisation has completed an audit does not mean that it can rest on its laurels. The auditing process should be part of the club's ongoing marketing strategy and a means of keeping the organisation working at an optimum level. It is an effective 'key' to what's going on in the organisation and may help management plan more effective strategies.

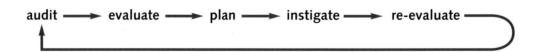

audit ⟶ evaluate ⟶ plan ⟶ instigate ⟶ re-evaluate ⟶

'Success or failure in the first instance does not guarantee the same thing will occur next time. Organisations need to understand that once a policy of including people with a disability in their activities has been adopted they must still work hard at making each individual case a success. Persistence is valuable in this area.'

How a club or organisation maintains this quality of service will vary given each individual circumstance. There are some basic checks you can implement that will help your club or organisation maintain the quality of service to members. Using the Active Australia Provider checklist criteria referring to 'quality of service', you can easily track how you are performing.

Table 10: Sample quality of service checklist

Quality of service	1	2	3	4	5	Evidence/action	Date achieved
1. Our aims and practices are directed toward satisfying our clients with disabilities.	X					There is nothing specifically directed at people with disabilities.	
2. We have appropriate procedures for our activities to ensure they are always carried out well.			X			Good general processes in place that ensure smooth running of club but need to address specific processes for people with disabilities.	
3. We continually review all aspects of our standard of service for the purpose of planning and improvement.				X		We do review processes within club through various committees but need to establish equity/ disability focus within structure.	
4. We involve all appropriate stakeholders in our reviews.				X		We have invited people with disabilities onto committees but at present have no representation.	
5. We have established good relationships with relevant local agencies.				X		Recently established liaison with State multi-disability agency and local generic disability groups.	

1 Have not considered   2 Thinking about it   3 Starting to develop   4 Implementing   5 Achieving and monitoring

By completing this simple checklist you can see whether you are providing good quality of service for people with disabilities (see Appendix 11 for a blank proforma).

3.5 Impressive doorknobs, shiny keys

Identifying specific marketing strategies to encourage people with a disability to join your organisation.

How can individuals and groups who might be potential customers be identified? How can you encourage people with disabilities to take a look behind the door and — even more importantly — stay and join you?

The organisation may have conducted an audit, educated the members, worked through physical access issues and have the welcome committee on standby, but not have attracted one person with a disability.

3.5.1 Target groups

If clubs wish to encourage people with disabilities to join they will need to think about proactive strategies. The organisation will need to think about who might want to join in their activities and how they can be best approached. This process must include deciding who may want to join your organisation and take part in the activities offered, deciding on the best approach, targeting a specific age, gender and demographic group and deciding, after consultation, how the product being offered will be developed.

Identify who you might approach

Most people who join your organisation will live locally. Look around and identify what organisations or individuals are located near you and approach them first. Occasionally, individuals from other areas may join if what you are offering is not offered in their area.

A good way to start is by checking if there is a specific group or body in your area which might be interested in working with you. Ask existing members for their ideas, look in the White Pages or ring your local council. It is all a matter of knocking on the right doors!

Contact individuals or organisations and ask what they want

People with a disability will only join your organisation if you meet a need.

Exploring what the person/people with a disability expect to gain is useful. After all, there is no point marketing a product heavily dependent on improved skills when people might just want to enjoy an activity while developing people and social skills.

Make the opportunity to talk to whoever you can to identify what in particular people with a disability are looking for that you might be able to provide.

> **Words from a club official**
>
> *'Although we'd looked at our club to see if it was suitable for people with disabilities and made appropriate changes we'd forgotten the most important thing — to tell them that we existed.'*

3.5.2 Develop your product

After consulting local groups, individuals and support groups, a clear picture of needs and expectations should evolve. This information should be regularly given out to new members and put together to produce a package that should be appealing to your new members with a disability. In the same way as any other membership package must be appealing, so must the material you develop for people with a disability. It should be value for money without being charity and should clearly meet the needs you identified in discussions earlier.

This package may include:

- support programs for all new members, ie a ' buddy' program

- information about 'come and try' days

- information about the activities

- information on minor modifications which have been made to physical facilities *(if any were needed)*

Not all people with a disability will want to participate in an organisation's activities. Just because you have marketed to a person with a disability doesn't mean you will get a response.

3.5.3 Reach out

Once you have developed your package you have to let people know where to go and how to get the package. The club will need to try a variety of ways to get the information to the target group.

- Use local radio stations for interviews and advertisements.

- Ask local papers for publicity and develop feature stories.

- Make presentations to individuals or to groups in larger organisations.

- Plan for 'come and try' days and family days targeting specific groups or local organisations.

- Work with local disability organisations.

- Remember to include the services provided to people with a disability in all club promotional brochures and material.

MARKETING YOUR CLUB AT A GLANCE...

Define the service — WHAT are you providing that is different, in demand, needed?

Settle the objectives — WHAT do you want to achieve for your club?

Define the target market — WHO, specifically, do you want to attract? Be very specific in terms of gender, age, skill level etc.

Develop the marketing strategy — HOW are you going to do this?

Compile the market plan — a useful and simple document that details exactly the action that your club is going to take, who is going to take it and when. It should also outline the resources that are needed.

Rahul and the Kingswool Tennis Club...

The Kingswool Tennis Club is a community club providing a range of competition opportunities regardless of age, gender or ability. The club was forced to have a good look at the implementation of their 'opportunities for all' philosophy after its membership dropped to a dangerous low. After much discussion it was decided that the club must tap into a previously untapped market. The members decided that they would approach the local special school and offer a tennis program for the students with intellectual disabilities in Year 7.

After prior planning and consultation with the school, it was decided that the students would be offered an eight-week program in a welcoming, friendly and non-threatening environment. Participants received expert coaching as well as encouragement in a friendly round-robin competition. After the program was finished, options available to the students included:

- integration into the club's mainstream competition

- integration into the club's other specialised group programs: the juniors, and the weekly women's programs

- continuation of the coaching program after school

- leaving the program at its conclusion without any penalty

As a result the club attracted eight new members including Rahul, who is extremely enthusiastic about his club and new-found friends. The club has benefited from more than just Rahul's membership fee, as his friendly attitude and willingness to help out have been a great asset to the club.

Section 4
Implications for sport and physical activity

Contents

4.1	Amputations	107
4.2	Asthma	108
4.3	Attention deficit hyperactivity disorder	111
4.4	Autism	114
4.5	Cancer	116
4.6	Cerebral palsy	119
4.7	Cystic fibrosis	122
4.8	Deafness and being hard of hearing	123
4.9	Diabetes	126
4.10	Down syndrome	129
4.11	Emotional disturbances	131
4.12	Epilepsy	133
4.13	HIV/AIDS and blood disorders	136
4.14	Juvenile rheumatoid arthritis and osteoporosis	137
4.15	Mental health	139
4.16	Muscular dystrophy	142
4.17	Obesity	144
4.18	Schizophrenia	145
4.19	Spina bifida	148
4.20	Spinal cord injuries	151
4.21	Transplants	153
4.22	Vision impairment	154

'To know is more important than to see, to understand is more important than to hear'

Implications for sport and physical activity

As a person who provides sport and/or physical activity opportunities for people with disabilities it is important that you understand some of the implications that the disability will have on your services. This is not to say that all disabilities will have implications for sport — many will not. It is a common misconception that knowledge of disability is the most important issue. It is often more important to understand and work with what the person can do, what their likes and dislikes are and how the planned activity may need adapting to their needs.

This section provides a basic overview of various conditions and their implications for sport and physical activity. There are also general guidelines to assist you in preparing your program to suit the specific needs of the individual. They may help you understand some of the medical and safety implications of certain conditions. Remember, however, that no two people with a specific disability will be the same. You will need to work with the individual to understand their needs.

4.1 Amputations

The term 'amputee' refers to people who have at least one major joint in a limb missing (ie elbow, wrist, knee or ankle) or — in cases where the amputation is through the joint — to people who have no functional movement at that joint. Amputations are either congenital or acquired. Congenital amputations occur as a result of a failure of the foetus to develop properly during the first three months of gestation. Acquired amputations can be the result of disease, trauma or tumour.

Classifications

The point of amputation and the portion of limb remaining will affect functional level. For example, someone with a below-the-knee amputation will require a leg prosthesis to walk. Flexion and extension are still possible, however, and he/she may have well developed quadriceps and control over lower extremities. The classes for amputees are:

A1	Double leg, above knee	A6	Single arm, above elbow
A2	Single leg, above knee	A7	Double arm, below elbow
A3	Double leg, below knee	A8	Single arm, below elbow
A4	Single leg, below knee	A9	Multiple combinations
A5	Double arm, above elbow		

Implications for physical activity

- It is important to encourage those people with an amputation to compete in sport or physical activity, even if it is only at a grassroots, non-competitive level, as this provides social interaction and support groups for students.

- Generally speaking, people with amputations are able to participate in activities to the same, or similar, levels as their able-bodied peers. Often few, if any, adaptations are needed to appropriately accommodate people with amputations.

- It is important to develop confidence in physical activity for the person with an amputation. Missing a limb can cause a distortion in body image; hence, goals for physical activity should be set that are easily achievable to increase confidence.

- Skin care around the stump area may be a problem. Periodic ventilation will help remove potential irritants or infections.

- The centre of gravity may be affected which in turn affects balance. This may improve as the individual gets used to the prosthetic device. Someone with an above-the-joint amputation will have more difficulty with balance because they lack the stability provided by the knee and/or elbow.

- There may be problems associated with thermoregulation for amputees. Because the amount of body surface for perspiration is reduced, the body may overheat on particularly hot or humid days. Monitor effort and performance and ensure plenty of liquids are taken before and during activity on these days.

- People with amputations may have experienced low levels of physical activity because of their amputation/attitude toward activity/parental protection. Programming should take into account the individual's present level of fitness when planning.

- Some people with amputation may avoid situations in which their difference is easily noticeable, such as in a swimming pool. Try to educate other teachers and students about the individual's condition to allay any fears or misconceptions regarding activity.

4.2   Asthma

Asthma is a condition in which the bronchial tubes narrow, causing mild to severe obstruction of the airway. The bronchial tubes become unusually sensitive to a variety of different 'triggers' (Goodman 1993), which cause:

- the swelling and inflammation of the mucus membranes

- the production of extra mucus that blocks the bronchiole tubes, and/or

- the tightening of the muscles of the bronchial tubes.

The narrowing of the bronchial tubes causes difficulty in breathing. Common trigger factors include animal fur or pollens, colds, exercise, environmental conditions such as cold winds or humidity, dust, smoke, some food substances and fumes. Childhood asthma can be distinguished from adult asthma, particularly in terms of how the young person reacts to various forms of medication. Childhood asthma can be categorised into three groups (Morton 1994):

1. Occasional episodic asthma
Occurs only 3–4 times a year and is usually associated with viral illness.

2. Episodic asthma
Occurs approximately monthly and is triggered by a variety of factors. Asthmatic 'episodes' can last up to a week and there are usually no residual symptoms.

3. Chronic persistent asthma

Acute attacks occur, sometimes over a period of months, and residual symptoms such as wheezing, chest tightness, the production of mucus and coughing are present.

The management and treatment of asthma involve the avoidance of trigger factors and the use of prescribed medication. Some trigger factors are easy to avoid, such as dust and fumes, but others are not easily avoided. Of major concern to teachers and sports leaders is the management of exercise-induced asthma. While physical activity can trigger an attack it is also of great benefit to asthmatics as exercise improves lung capacity.

Medical treatment of asthma

There are three types of medication used to treat asthma:

Relievers (short-acting bronchodilators)

Reliever medications work by relaxing the muscles around the airways to relieve the blockage in the airways. Relievers usually bring quick relief from asthma symptoms. Can be used for premedication before exercise and for rapid relief of symptoms.

Preventors (inhaled corticosteroids and nonsteroidal medications)

Preventor medications are anti-inflammatory and work to reduce airway sensitivity and prevent attacks from occurring. These medications work long term and need to be taken as prescribed. Leukotriene receptor antagonists tend to work well in people with exercise-induced asthma.

Symptom controllers (long-acting bronchodilators)

These medications help to relax the muscles of the tightened airways. Their effect usually lasts for up to 12 hours. They should not be used for immediate relief in an asthma attack. It is of benefit for those who experience exercise-induced asthma. They should always be used along with a preventor — not on their own.

Exercise-induced asthma

Exercise-induced asthma is very common among school age children. The intensity and duration of exercise are important factors in the management of exercise-induced asthma. While all forms of exercise may trigger an attack, prolonged exercise such as running, rather than stop/start activities, is more likely to cause it. Exercise-induced asthma generally becomes more severe after exercise as the body cools but can also occur during exercise, usually precipitated by symptoms such as wheezing, coughing and constantly clearing the throat.

If an acute asthma attack does occur it is important to know how to deal with it. Table 11 presents some general guidelines on dealing with an acute asthma attack.

When proper precautions are taken and medication is administered effectively, asthma is not a barrier to participation in physical activity.

Implications for physical activity

- Activities such as swimming are particularly good for young people with asthma, as warm, humid air is less likely to cause exercise-induced asthma. Avoid sudden changes in temperature (warm body into cold water).

> **Table 11:** Dealing with an acute asthma attack
>
> 1. In people with episodic asthma and a known trigger factor allow the person to use the prescribed medication 5–10 minutes before exercise.
> 2. Allow the person to use prescribed medication as soon as possible.
> 3. NEVER encourage the person to 'run through' an attack.
> 4. Be aware of the person's medical history for details of medication.
> 5. Help the person to relax by keeping calm and avoiding panic. The anxiety caused by the person's breathlessness may be made worse if those around are not calm.
> 6. If facilities are available, run a hot shower and allow the person to breathe moist, warm air.
> 7. If the symptoms do not respond after 2 or 3 doses of medication, seek medical help.
>
> NB: Delay in treating the attack will make the condition more difficult to treat.

- Short-burst activities such as softball and volleyball are preferable, and be sure to incorporate good warm-up/cool-down periods before and after exercise. Experiment with duration and intensity of exercise until you understand the likely level of activity most comfortable for the individual.

- Make sure there are opportunities to rest during activities.

- Keep play areas/gyms clean and free of dust as much as possible.

- Discuss the condition with the individual and with his/her parents. Record trigger factors, likely symptoms or warning signs on a simple pro forma — it will be useful for others as well.

- The intake of medication during exercise may be needed — allow the young person to stop and use his/her 'puffer'. An extra puff may be necessary within a few minutes to reverse an attack.

- Remind people about the need for medication before activity if necessary.

- Activities that emphasise breathing control, such as karate and dance, are also recommended.

First aid for asthma

Step one

Sit the person comfortably upright. Be calm and reassuring.

Step two

Give four puffs of a blue **reliever** inhaler (puffer) — Ventolin, Airsmir, Bricanyl or Asmol.

Relievers are best given through a spacer. Use one puff at a time and ask the person to take four breaths from the spacer after each puff.

Step three

Wait four minutes. If there is no improvement give another four puffs.

Step four

If there is no improvement, call an ambulance immediately, and state that the person is having an asthma attack. Continue giving the person four puffs every four minutes until the ambulance arrives.

Children: **4 puffs each time is a safe dose.**

Adults: **up to 6–8 puffs every five minutes may be given for a severe attack while waiting for the ambulance.**

4.3   Attention deficit hyperactivity disorder

Attention deficit hyperactivity disorder (ADHD) is thought to be a form of brain damage, though the cause of the brain damage is unknown. There is growing consensus that children with ADHD have an inherent biologically determined temperament predisposing them to ADHD symptoms. Other explanations for the disorder include insufficient chemicals in the brain called neurotransmitters, which carry messages between the brain cells. If the brain cannot communicate effectively, the child cannot focus and organise intellectual resources.

There are three basic behavioural patterns that distinguish a child with ADHD from one without it. These are:

* inattention

* hyperactivity

* impulsivity

While many children experience outbursts of ADHD-type behaviour, children with the disorder experience it at a much more frequent and severe rate. Young people with ADHD are characteristically about four years behind their developmental stage in some areas but not in others.

Potential problems associated with ADHD

Common characteristics of children with ADHD include sudden temper outbursts, rapid mood swings, refusal to cooperate or being too quiet or too loud. Some children with ADHD may appear inactive or disengaged due to inattention. Often children with ADHD experience other forms of mental illness and behavioural disorders. Intellectual and social development may be hindered by the disorder.

As children with ADHD mature, their symptoms tend to become less obvious. Children may experience feelings of restlessness and jitteriness instead of feeling a need to run everywhere and climb over objects.

Diagnostic Criteria for Attention Deficit Hyperactivity Disorder

Children with ADHD are usually assessed against two basic sets of criteria (A1 and A2):

A. 1. Six or more of the following symptoms of inattention, which have persisted for at least six months:

Inattention

— often fails to give close attention to details, making careless mistakes in schoolwork or other activities

— often has difficulty sustaining attention or concentration in tasks or social activity

— often appears to be distracted, not hearing what has been said

— often has trouble executing instructions or requests and fails to complete any started task

— often has difficulty organising tasks or activities

— often avoids or dislikes tasks which demand sustained concentration or mental effort

— often loses things necessary for task

— is easily distracted by irrelevant stimuli

— is often forgetful in daily activities

2. Six or more of the following symptoms of hyperactivity-impulsivity, which have persisted for at least six months:

Hyperactivity

— often fidgets with hands or feet or squirms in seat

— often leaves seat at inappropriate times

— often runs or climbs on things excessively

— often has difficulty playing in quiet activities

— is often on the go, unable to sit still

— often talks excessively

Impulsivity

— often blurts out answers before questions have been completed

— is often impatient, unable to wait their turn

— often interrupts or intrudes on others at inappropriate times.

B. Some hyperactive-impulsive or inattentive symptoms that caused impairment were present before the age of seven years

C. Some impairments from the symptoms are present in at least two separate situations ie at home and at school

D. There must be clear evidence of clinically significant impairment in social, academic and occupational functioning

E. The symptoms do not occur exclusively during the course of a pervasive developmental disorder, schizophrenia, or other psychotic disorder and are not accounted for by some other mental disorder

There are three sorts of attention deficit hyperactivity disorder:

1. ADHD Combined Type: have at least six symptoms of inattention and at least six symptoms of hyperactivity-impulsivity for at least six months beforehand

2. ADHD Predominantly Inattentive Type: at least six symptoms of inattention but not six symptoms of hyperactivity-impulsivity for at least six months beforehand

3. ADHD Predominantly Hyperactivity-Impulsivity Type: at least six symptoms of hyperactivity-impulsivity but not six symptoms of inattention for at least six months beforehand

It is important to remember that not all children who experience some of the above behaviour are necessarily subject to ADHD. There are numerous tests and procedures to take before the child can or will be diagnosed with this disorder.

Behaviour management

Children with ADHD do not understand their actions and are not in control of their own behaviour. It is therefore necessary for adults to help shape their behaviour for them. Some of the following tips may be useful for parents and teachers:

- praise good behaviour immediately

- praise randomly — for normal things that other children might do automatically

- praise appropriate behaviour often

- be specific about what they have done correctly or successfully, and

- ignore harmless or nuisance behaviour.

Implications for physical activity

- Create routine, regularity and repetition.

- Be aware that many children with ADHD will be on some form of medication, usually stimulants. These will slow the child down and may cause side-effects of depressed appetites and sleeplessness. Sherrill (1993) suggests that these medications may affect coordination and balance.

- Reward children for appropriate behaviour.

- Try teaching children with ADHD in areas where there are minimal distractions.

- Examples of strong prompts may be useful in gaining attention.

- Encourage children to perform movements slowly: how slowly can you do a forward roll? Incorporate relaxation exercises into physical activity. For example, 'tense your leg, hold it, and relax. Feel how loose your leg has become.' These techniques will help a child learn the feeling of 'slow' and 'relaxed' rather than 'fast' and 'tense'.

- A buddy system may help the child to remain focused and attentive for longer periods of time.

- Use strategies to help focus on skills to be learnt. When breaking a skill down (using task analysis) reinforce each part of the skill by using verbal repetition, markers and miming.

- Avoid comparison with other children. Recognise good performance and reward 'most improved' individuals.

4.4 Autism

Autism is a form of brain damage that affects the development of the brain. It is thought to be associated with neurological and biological deficiencies. Children with autism will have problems in several areas of their development. As a result, people with autism have a hindered ability to relate to the outside world; they are often unable to communicate, and their behavioural and social skills are usually inappropriate for someone of their age. The cause of the brain damage is unknown. Autism usually presents itself during the first three years of a child's life and will remain for the duration of the child's life.

There is no cure for autism, but as medical professionals have become more educated and aware of the disorder, strategies which help a person with autism to cope better and lead a productive life have been developed.

Recognising autism

People who are autistic display a great variety of behavioural characteristics. The list below presents some typical characteristics of autism. While these may be typical no one person will possess all the characteristics, but may have some of them at various levels of severity.

People with autism will display at least half of the characteristics listed below. However, each person will have a different level of severity of a particular characteristic, or a different combination of the behavioural patterns.

- difficulty mixing with other people

- inappropriate laughing and giggling

- little or no eye contact

- apparent insensitivity to pain

- prefers to be alone; aloof manner

- spins objects

- inappropriate attachment to objects

- noticeable physical overactivity or extreme underactivity

- unresponsive to normal teaching methods

- uneven gross or fine motor skills (may not be able to kick a football but can stack blocks)

- tantrums — displays extreme distress for no apparent reason

- difficulty in expressing needs; uses gestures or pointing instead of words

- not responsive to verbal cues; acts as deaf

- may not want cuddling or act cuddly

- repeats phrases or words instead of normal language

- sustained odd play

- no real fear of dangers

- insistence on sameness; resists changes in routine

About 70% of young people with autism have some degree of intellectual disability. Generally speaking, however, young people with autism display very distinct characteristics and have to painstakingly learn patterns of speech and appropriate ways to relate to people, objects and events. The American Psychiatric Association and the World Health Organization have developed formal classifications of autistic behaviour.

Types of autism

- Autistic Disorder — children with this disorder display impairments in social interaction, communication and creative playing up to three years of age. They have stereotyped behaviours, interests and activities.

- Aspergers Disorder — these people display a high level of intelligence and have no significant delay of language skills. There are limitations in social interaction, behaviour and the presence of restricted interests and activities.

- Pervasive Developmental Disorder — Not Otherwise Specified — these children display autistic characteristics but do not exhibit the behaviour patterns for specific diagnosis.

- Rett's Disorder — at present this disorder is only found in females; the onset of the disorder is at 1–4 years of age. This disorder is characterised by a period of normal development, then a sudden loss of previously acquired skills. Repetitive hand movements replace normal hand movements.

- Childhood Disintegrative Disorder — a child with this disorder will have progressed and developed normally for a period of up to two years of age before losing acquired skills.

Implications for physical activity

- The types of activities suitable for people with autism will depend on age and the severity of the condition. Generally speaking, the older the individual the more important it is to develop functional skills, while the younger the individual the more important it is to develop basic skills such as balance and coordination.

- Create very structured daily learning environments. Visual processing is usually more effective for young people with autism than auditory processing.

- There is a great need to individualise your program to suit the unique needs of the young person.

- Think about the transition between activities. Create a home base to act as a reference point for the individual. Use visual or auditory cues to signal specific movements between one activity and another.

- Try to gauge change in the daily environment for the individual. From time to time subtly change the environment to discourage stereotypical behaviours.

- The development of functional gross motor skills is particularly important for children with autism. Remember that patience is required and progress may seem slow.

- Repeat simple visual demonstrations, use short and succinct terms to describe activities and manually guide the individual in the early stages of skill development.

- Food reinforcers have often been used as reward for appropriate behaviour in therapy programs for individuals with autism. However, it's better to use more appropriate age-related reinforcers, such as applause or 'gold stars'.

4.5 Cancer

Cancer is a disease which affects the growth of the body's cells due to alterations in the genes of the cells. Cancer is the term given to any disease which may be malignant; it can affect any part of the body. It develops when the cells of the body start to grow and behave abnormally. The cells start to multiply rapidly and may form a lump or mass.

The lump or growth may be benign (non-cancerous) or malignant (cancerous). If the growth continues it may invade other tissue in the body, including the lymph nodes and bloodstream, and thus spread the cancer. These secondary growths are known as metastases.

The cause of cancer is as yet unknown, but some factors are considered to act as a catalyst for the development of cancer. Some of these factors are exposure to tobacco, UV radiation from the sun, industrial chemicals and viruses, and a genetic predisposition.

Cancer can affect children as well as adults. The most common types of cancer affecting children include:

- leukaemia
- lymphoma
- brain/nerve tumour
- retinoblastoma
- Wilm's tumour
- sarcoma

Leukaemia

Leukaemia accounts for one third of all childhood cancers. Most of these cancers are acute lymphoblastic leukaemias, whose cause is still unknown. Leukaemia occurs when your body develops abnormally functioning white blood cells, reducing the number of mature white blood cells and the number of platelets and red blood cells. Leukaemia cells are abnormal because they cannot mature properly, in that they do not die and cannot be used up.

Leukaemia cells multiply in the bone marrow, where the healthy bone marrow is replaced by leukaemia cells. As a result of this there are not enough red blood cells to carry oxygen around the body, there are not enough mature white blood cells to fight infection and there are not enough platelets to stop any bleeding.

Signs and symptoms of leukaemia

A child is likely to feel generally unwell, and may complain of aching and painful limbs and swollen glands. Because leukaemia cells multiply in the bone marrow, the development of normal red blood cells may slow, causing the child to become tired and lethargic due to the lack of red blood cells and the possible development of anaemia. Bruises may develop and bleeding may occur. The child could become more susceptible to infections because of low numbers of white blood cells.

Lymphoma

Lymphomas are a type of cancer that has originated in the lymphatic system of the body. The lymphatic system is the body's natural defence against infection. It is made up of a collection of glands (nodes) situated throughout the body including the neck, armpits, chest, abdomen and groin. The tonsils and spleen also are part of the lymphatic system.

There are two types of lymphomas, Hodgkin's and non-Hodgkin's (NHL). Both types can often be cured, though the treatment is different.

Signs and symptoms of lymphomas

Initially there may be some swelling in the lymph nodes, particularly the neck area. This swelling is usually painless, but it may affect other bodily functions. For example, swelling in the chest area may cause breathlessness or a persistent cough, and swelling in the abdomen may lead to bowel obstruction.

Other symptoms include fever, tiredness, weight loss and loss of appetite. In NHL children, the bone marrow and spinal cord fluid may be affected.

Brain tumours

Brain tumours are the most common types of tumour affecting children and the third most prevalent type of childhood cancer. The cause of a brain tumour is unknown, but it can affect any part of the brain. Brain tumours are not likely to spread to other parts of the body. However, they can invade the normal brain tissue surrounding it, thus indirectly affecting other bodily function.

Signs and symptoms of brain tumours

Because the skull is a closed environment, the development of a brain tumour increases the intracranial pressure inside the skull. This results in headaches, feeling and/or being sick and drowsiness. Children may become irritable and lose interest in school and normal activities. Occasionally a person may experience fits or a loss of consciousness. Increased pressure in the skull also happens if the flow of the cerebrospinal fluid is blocked. This fluid surrounds the brain and spinal cord. If this happens in a young baby, the soft spot on the top of the head may bulge and the head may increase in size.

Retinoblastoma

Retinoblastoma occurs in the light-sensitive lining of the eye known as the retina. It can occur in two forms, either with tumours in both eyes (inherited form) or in one eye only (non-inherited form).

In inherited tumours, the person affected usually has a genetic abnormality, passed from parent to child. Patients with this gene, known as the Rb gene, have a greater susceptibility to developing other tumours outside the eye.

The cause of non-inherited tumours is unknown.

Signs and symptoms of retinoblastoma

If there is a family history of retinoblastoma the baby is checked for the disease soon after birth. For those children with no family history of the disease, the first thing that is noticed is a white pupil that does not reflect light. If the tumour is large it may cause a painful red eye.

Wilm's tumour (nephroblastoma)

Wilm's tumour is a cancer that affects the person's kidneys. It is most common in children under five years of age. All developing babies posses specialised cells known as nephroblasts, which are involved in the development of the kidneys. These cells usually disappear at birth. In children with Wilm's tumour, these cells are still present after birth.

The cause of Wilm's tumour is still unknown. However, some children with this type of cancer may have a non-hereditary disease or illness present at birth. Examples of these abnormalities include a lack of an iris in the eye, or abnormalities of the genitals; sometimes one side of a child's body may be slightly bigger than the other side.

Signs and symptoms of Wilm's tumour

Swelling of the abdomen is the most common symptom of Wilm's tumour. It is usually painless, unless there has been some bleeding from the tumour, which may cause some abdominal pain if touched. There may be blood in the child's urine and their blood pressure may be high. Other symptoms include a fever, weight loss, loss of appetite or a stomach upset.

Sarcoma

This type of cancer can develop in any part of the body. It usually starts in a bone, most commonly the bones of the hips, upper arm or thigh. Sarcomas are typically bone cancers, but in some instances the cancer may spread to soft tissue surrounding the bone. In some instances a sarcoma can develop initially in the soft tissue. The most common form of soft tissue sarcoma is rhabdomyosarcoma, found mainly in the head and neck areas.

Signs and symptoms of sarcomas

People with sarcoma tend to feel pain in the affected bone. There may be some swelling in the area and it is painful to touch. As the cancer progresses the person may develop a fever.

Skin cancer

It has been found that exposure to sun at an early age may increase the chances of skin damage and perhaps even skin cancer, in particular melanoma. There are numerous precautionary steps that can be taken to minimise the risk of such conditions.

Implications for physical activity — skin cancer

- Understand the rationale for morning sport, when the sun is less dangerous and exposure may be safer.

- Ensure that the children slip on a shirt with a high neckline and longer sleeves.

- Provide sunscreen SPF 30+ for all the children. Apply this at least 20 minutes before the commencement of sporting activities, and reapply every two hours or more unless the sunscreen has been wiped off earlier.

- Incorporate sun hats into the school or club uniform. A wide-brimmed hat offers the greatest protection for children.

- Use the shade whenever you can.

- Positive role models will help to change attitudes toward sun protection.

Implications for physical activity — general

- Ensure that there is permission from the child's doctor for appropriate sports or physical activities.

- Remember that each child is different, and at a different stage of treatment. Modify programs or sports to cater for the child's needs and abilities.

- Take into account the cancer of the child — be aware of possible dangers to the child when playing sport. For example, children with a low platelet count may be advised to take caution or avoid contact sport, as intense contact may cause internal bleeding resulting in serious illness or death.

- Be aware that during aerobic exercise fatigue could be a major factor.

- Due to a loss of appetite and tiredness energy levels may be low.

4.6   Cerebral palsy

Cerebral palsy is a central neurological condition. It is an inclusive term which covers a group of motor disorders, such as disorders of movement and posture which are associated with a defect, injury or damage to the developing brain (eg occurring in children under five years). It is a non-progressive condition that may originate before, during, or after birth, and which manifests itself in a loss or impairment of control over voluntary musculature (Winnick 1990).

Up to 20% of children with cerebral palsy acquire the condition after birth. For the rest the condition was present at birth, the result of a congenital defect. Although there is no known cause of cerebral palsy, research shows that certain factors may contribute to the development of this condition. Head injuries or brain illness are contributing factors for those children who have acquired the disease, while prematurity, jaundice, stroke/intracranial haemorrhage and perinatal asphyxia may be significant in the development of cerebral palsy at birth.

Types of cerebral palsy

There are three main types of cerebral palsy; it can affect one limb, two limbs or all the limbs.

1 Spastic Cerebral Palsy

This type of cerebral palsy is the most common accounting for approximately 80% of all cerebral palsy diagnosis. People with this type of cerebral palsy have an increase in muscle tone — their muscles become quite rigid and feel stiff and tight. Coordination of these muscles is lost, as some muscles become overactive and others become underactive. This causes inaccurate voluntary motion. There are three types of spasticity:

- Spastic hemiplegia — this is the most common form of cerebral palsy and usually involves one arm and one leg on one side of the body.

- Spastic quadriplegia — all four limbs are affected by spasticity. This is the most severe type of cerebral palsy.

- Spastic diplegia — the lower limbs are more affected than the upper limbs. Hands and arms have poor coordination but otherwise normal function.

2 Athetosis or Diskinetic Cerebral Palsy

People with this type of cerebral palsy have variable muscle tone: sometimes their muscles will be tight, other times they will be unable to control their posture and stability. Occasionally if a person is upset involuntary jerking movements occur especially in the fingers and wrist. All four limbs are affected to varying degrees by athetosis.

3 Ataxic Cerebral Palsy

A person's balance and orientation are affected by this type of cerebral palsy. The muscles are quite loose and there is low muscle tone. There is poor coordination in general, resulting in an awkwardness of movements.

Mixed types

Some people have a mixture of the different types of cerebral palsy, the most common combination being spasticity and athetosis.

Potential problems associated with cerebral palsy

- Muscle contracture — fragile muscles which become difficult to move because of the muscle's resistance to lengthening. Weak muscles may lead to scoliosis because of their inability to support bones and joints

- Persistence of primitive reflexes — common in children with severe disability. The most typical forms of this reflex include:

  — the Moro reflex: a sudden backward reflex of the head and upper body with the arms stretching sideways

  — the asymmetric tonic neck reflex: occurs when the head is turned to the side. The arms and legs on that side extend, whilst the opposing limbs flex

  — the positive support reflex: the whole body stiffens

- Gastro-oesophageal reflux — acid from the stomach leaks back up into the gullet

- Bowel and bladder problems — caused by many factors including inadequate diet, dependence on others to get to the bathroom, increased abdominal muscle contraction and uncoordination of the bladder muscles

- Emotional and behaviour problems

- Vision problems — the most common being squinting or a turn in the eye. Eye problems develop in about half of the children with cerebral palsy

- Intellectual disability

- Epilepsy — occurs in one-third of all children with cerebral palsy

- Deafness — affects approximately 7% of children with cerebral palsy

- Perceptual difficulties — these may cause learning difficulties

- Problems with communication, language, eating and swallowing may be present

- Hydrocephalus — caused by a build-up of fluid in the brain

Implications for physical activity

- People with cerebral palsy are affected by greater fatigue during tasks where speed and organisation is required. This may affect fine motor control and perceptual abilities. Ensure that children with cerebral palsy are not pushed beyond their physical threshold and allow time for recovery.

- Communication may be a problem if speech impairments are also present. Patience and understanding are required.

- Many activities require either central control or control to distal movements. If the head and trunk are affected this will complicate the individual's ability to perform certain tasks. Be aware that although certain major limbs may be the most affected, such as the lower body in diplegia cerebral palsy, simple fine motor skills such as grasping can also have a significant impact on motor performance.

- Developmental and corrective exercises may be incorporated into activity programs — it is important that individuals with cerebral palsy are provided with the opportunity to develop their functional levels within the activity program. For example, it is easy to incorporate stretching flexor group movements for individuals with spastic cerebral palsy or relaxation, coordination and balance exercises for individuals with athetosis and ataxia cerebral palsy.

- Head and/or trunk dysfunction, no matter how mild, will affect sitting position, standing position and most movement patterns.

- Be aware that it is important for people with spastic cerebral palsy that muscle imbalance at affected joints is worked on when possible. Try relaxing tight muscles so that weak antagonist muscles are contracted. Work with the individual so that he/she begins to feel variations in muscle tone. Do not be frustrated, as this will take time.

- Generally speaking, people with cerebral palsy should be more successful in activities that involve larger muscle groups, such as running, throwing or jumping. Practising fine motor skills may lead to frustration — work on these on an individual basis before introducing them into group activities.

- Encourage appropriate technique but allow for the individual to develop his/her own way of doing things. Functional ability is more important than style — work with the individual to decide upon the most appropriate methods.

- Balance exercises are important — do not be discouraged or be overprotective if the individual falls over a lot in the beginning. Persist and practise!

- People with spastic cerebral palsy need careful positioning. Be aware that sudden excitement, fear, tiredness and/or loud noises may aggravate the spasticity and lead to a sudden 'startle' reflex.

4.7 Cystic fibrosis

Cystic fibrosis is an inherited genetic condition which mainly affects the lungs, digestive system and sweat glands. It is the most common life-threatening condition affecting Australian children.

The mucus of people with cystic fibrosis is unusually thick and sticky. This gradually causes lung damage and a loss of lung function. There is also an increased likelihood of infections such as pneumonia as bacteria collects in the mucus. The build-up of mucus can also plug up the pancreatic ducts, preventing digestive enzymes from reaching the small intestine which results in digestive problems and undernourishment.

With improvements in medical technology, life expectancy for individuals with cystic fibrosis has improved in recent years. The most common cause of death is respiratory failure due to lung damage. The symptoms and severity of cystic fibrosis vary markedly from relatively little impairment to severely impaired health.

The management and treatment of cystic fibrosis usually entail a mixture of medication and dietary control. To help strengthen the immune system and to counter undernourishment, dietary supplements in the form of extra calories, proteins and multivitamins are often prescribed. Prolonged use of antibiotics is sometimes necessary to counter pulmonary infections and oral bronchodilators are used to help reverse airway obstruction. 'Pulmonary therapy' helps clear the lungs and involves various forms of postural drainage, such as chest massage, vibration and percussion.

Symptoms of cystic fibrosis

People with cystic fibrosis may have some of the following ailments:

- a persistent cough

- difficulty breathing

- loss of appetite

- increase in urination

- fatigue or lethargy and a decrease in physical performance

- muscle cramps due to extensive loss of salt through sweating

Implications for physical activity

- Exercise as part of the regular daily routine is encouraged for people with cystic fibrosis. Research has indicated that there is a link between regular exercise and the survival of a person with cystic fibrosis.

- The perspiration of people with cystic fibrosis has a higher than normal salt content. Salt tablets will probably be required during vigorous physical activity. Check with the person or with his/her parents if these are required.

- Cystic fibrosis patients do not tolerate heat stress well, due to the high salt content in their sweat and consequent dehydration. Ensure that a person with cystic fibrosis drinks lots of water during exercise to avoid dehydration.

- Make sure you know what medications are being taken and understand their implications for physical activity. Some may be on medication that needs to be taken during exercise.

- Try to discuss the condition with other members of the group. People with cystic fibrosis sometimes need to cough out mucus in their lungs. Allow them to do this without appearing to be unnecessarily 'vulgar' to the rest of the group.

- The diet of the young person with cystic fibrosis may be different from others and as such the individual may have limited stamina. Allow for rest periods.

4.8 Deafness and being hard of hearing

'Deafness' usually refers to a hearing loss which renders it impossible to understand speech through hearing alone, even if a hearing aid is used. Usually an alternative or assistive mode of communication is required in order to communicate with a deaf person (eg lip-reading, signing, demonstrations or written messages) (Bremner and Goodman 1992).

Being 'hard of hearing' usually refers to a hearing loss that results in the understanding of speech being difficult, but not impossible (Bremner and Goodman 1992).

There are basically two measurements used to describe auditory levels, *pitch* and *intensity*. Pitch refers to the highness or lowness of sound. Intensity refers to the loudness or softness of sound. Degrees of hearing loss are measured with use of an audiogram and are described in decibels (dB). The various categories of hearing loss are presented in Table 12.

Table 12: Degrees of hearing loss

Degree of Impairment	Hearing threshold	Implications
Slight	27–40 dB	No significant difficulty even with faint speech.
Mild or hard of hearing	41–55 dB	Difficulty with only faint speech. With proper use of hearing aids the individual can usually function as well as a hearing person.
Moderate	56–70 dB	Frequent difficulty even with loud speech. Speech may be affected. May need good lip-reading and listening conditions to understand what is being said.
Severe	71–90 dB	Can perceive only shouted or amplified speech but may not necessarily understand it. May not have clear speech and may have some difficulty in following conversation. Good eye contact and clear articulation will assist understanding.
Profound	91+ dB	Usually cannot understand even amplified speech. May not have understandable speech and may use sign language to communicate. Will require face to face communication with good eye contact and may understand parts of messages through lip-reading. Gestures and demonstrations will assist communication.

NB: Ordinary conversation usually takes place in the 40–50 dB range.

Methods of communication

There are three basic methods of communication for people who are deaf. These are sign language, lip-reading and speech.

Sign language

This is a process of presenting words and phrases through hand signals, gestures, facial expressions and body movements. The two forms of sign language used in Australia are 'signed English' and 'Australian sign language' (Auslan). These forms are supplemented by finger spelling.

Signed English

This is a form of communication that is mostly used for educational purposes. It involves using a manual sign for every spoken word in the same order as would be used for spoken English. When there is no sign for the word then the word is finger spelt.

Auslan

This is a popular form of communication, separate from English, used in the Australian deaf community. It involves using signs to represent words, concepts and sometimes whole phrases. Auslan places emphasis on facial and whole body language in order to add expression and provide inflection.

Auslan is a very practical form of communication for people who are deaf. It is specific to the environment in which it is being used, that is, different signs which have the same meaning, are used within different regions of Australia. People of different ages use Auslan in different ways. (See 'Contacts/help' to obtain a copy of the Auslan dictionary from Deafness Resources.)

Lip-reading

Lip-reading is a form of communication used by some deaf people; it involves understanding spoken messages through observing the lip movements and reading the facial expressions of someone speaking to them. People with less severe hearing loss and a reasonable level of residual hearing are more likely to develop lip-reading skills. It is worth noting, however, that even those who are skilled lip-readers understand only a relatively small proportion of words in a conversation, approximately 30%.

People with post-lingual deafness (deafness that occurred after the development of speech and language) are more likely to develop lip-reading skills than those with pre-lingual deafness (deafness that was present at birth or originated at an age before speech and language developed).

Speech

A large proportion of people who are deaf comprehend some oral language through the use of a hearing aid, lip-reading and/or reading facial expressions. Many also use speech to communicate.

Types of hearing loss

It is important to understand the three major types of hearing loss. The three types are *conductive, sensorineural* and *mixed*. It is important because the type of hearing loss will influence the mode of communication employed for a particular individual.

Conductive hearing loss

Generally, people with conductive hearing loss require sounds that are louder than normal to restore normal or near-normal hearing. Conductive hearing loss may be due to:

- wax blockage in the ear canal

- perforation of the ear drum

- middle ear infections

- damage to tiny bones in the middle ear due to trauma

- genetic conditions, and/or

- ear, nose or throat problems or disease

Usually conductive hearing loss is temporary and can be corrected with hearing aids and/or medical or surgical treatment.

Sensorineural hearing loss

Young people with sensorineural hearing loss require clear and well-articulated speech patterns to help restore sound to normal or near-normal levels. Sounds are generally distorted and garbled. Increases in volume will not necessarily be of any benefit to young people with sensorineural hearing loss. This type of hearing loss may be due to:

- genetic conditions

- excessive noise exposure

- ageing

- illness such as meningitis

- toxic medications and trauma

Sensorineural hearing loss is more serious than conductive hearing loss and cannot necessarily be corrected through hearing aids or medical or surgical treatment.

Mixed hearing loss

This simply refers to a combination of both conductive and sensorineural hearing loss.

Implications for physical activity

- For conductive hearing loss minimal modifications are needed for individuals who use hearing aids. Environments with little background noise are good. Demonstrations or gestures may be needed in environments where hearing aids cannot be worn (eg swimming pools).

- For sensorineural and mixed hearing loss, become familiar with some basic signing skills. Some individuals, however, will rely more on lip-reading in conjunction with their residual hearing for communication and may be unable to sign (these people are sometimes referred to as the 'oral deaf').

- Visual demonstration is very important. Get to know the preferred methods of communication for each individual.

- Face the group you are talking to, think about group organisation (does the person with hearing impairment need to be at the front of the group?) and try not to stand with the sun or a bright light behind you when talking.

- Do not exaggerate lip movement, try to speak as clearly as possible.

- Be aware that hearing aids may not always be working effectively or may even be switched off. There is some evidence to suggest that some hearing impaired children hear better on some days than on others (Wiseman 1994).

- People with hearing impairment may expend more effort to hear than their peers. This may cause a degree of mental and emotional fatigue.

- Develop activities that foster social skills. Some young people with hearing impairment fail to develop adequate social skills because of their speech impairment.

4.9 Diabetes

Diabetes is a chronic condition. It is the result of the body's own immune system attacking the pancreas and destroying the body's insulin-making cells. Because the body is unable to absorb the sugar into its cells, the blood sugar level increases resulting in an overload of blood glucose. There are two types of diabetes: insulin dependent diabetes (Type 1) and non-insulin dependent diabetes (Type 2).

Type 1 diabetes

Type 1 diabetes occurs when the pancreas does not produce enough insulin. Insulin is used to allow the absorption of sugar into the body's cells to be used as energy. People who have diabetes do not produce enough insulin thus the sugar has no way of being absorbed by the body. When the sugar cannot be absorbed into the body's cells, it overflows into the kidneys and is excreted in the urine. Type 1 diabetes is most common among children and young adults.

Symptoms of Type 1 diabetes
- lethargy
- weight loss
- increased urination
- excessive thirst

Causes of Type 1 diabetes
Eating too much sugar does not cause diabetes. There are three factors that are thought to be significant in the development of Type 1 diabetes:

- inherited (genetic) factors;
- self allergy (auto-immunity); and
- environmental damage (virus or chemicals).

Treatment of Type 1 diabetes includes several injections of insulin per day as well as an eating plan. The insulin lowers blood sugar levels to the level considered normal. It is important that people with diabetes eat at the same time every day, as they must try and maintain a constant blood glucose level.

Type 2 diabetes

Occurs mainly in obese teenagers and overweight adults over 40 years of age. People with Type 2 diabetes still produce normal levels of insulin, but this insulin is not helpful in allowing the body to absorb sugar. Treatment of this type of diabetes does not involve insulin injections. A change of lifestyle including weight loss, healthier eating habits and perhaps a non-insulin pill will suffice.

Possible problems associated with diabetes

Almost all major organs in the body are damaged by diabetes. Some of the most serious complications associated with diabetes include:

- kidney failure

- nerve damage and loss of sensation in the extremities

- arteriosclerosis (hardening of the arteries) which can lead to heart disease and loss of extremities

- loss of sight

The importance of sport and physical activity

People with diabetes should be encouraged to participate in sport and physical activity because it:

- improves fitness and well-being

- encourages a lifelong healthy lifestyle

- builds self confidence and self esteem

- improves the action of insulin and enhances blood glucose control

Implications for physical activity

- Exercise is important for a person with diabetes. Exercising muscles use more glucose for energy, thus lowering blood glucose levels during and after exercise.

- Sometimes exercise makes the blood glucose levels go up.

- Food and drinks for the treatment of hypoglycaemia need to be available at the place of physical activity and sport.

- Students with diabetes need additional supervision during exercise. The younger persons may need their meals supervised before the onset of exercise.

- Allow the person to carry some high energy food, in case of a sudden hypo attack.

- Any sport in which a hypo could place the person in danger, should be modified to ensure safety.

- Water sports need very careful planning and supervision because a hypo increases the risk of drowning and some features of hypoglycaemia may be masked by the cooler body temperature experienced during a water based activity.

- Be aware that insulin is absorbed more readily in the exercising muscles (ie arms and legs). A good place to inject insulin before exercise is in the stomach or buttocks.

- The length of the exercising period will determine the amount of insulin needed by the person. For longer periods of exercise more carbohydrates and less insulin may be required, whereas short high intensity exercise periods may not require any alteration at all.

- If appropriate, measure blood glucose before exercise begins; this will also help determine the amount of insulin required by the person.

First aid for diabetic hyperglycaemia

Hyperglycaemia is when there is too much blood glucose in the bloodstream. Not enough insulin has been produced to adequately remove the glucose from the blood into the cells. This may be the result of eating too much, being sick or being stressed.

Signs that a person may be suffering from high blood glucose levels include:

- frequent urination

- excessive thirst

- weight loss

- lethargy

- change in behaviour

These are also the signs of undiagnosed Type 1 diabetes.

Hypoglycaemia

When there is not enough blood glucose, the brain is deprived of oxygen. Hypoglycaemia (as opposed to *hyperglycaemia*) occurs if there is too much insulin in the body as a result of exercise or not enough food.

Treatment of hypoglycaemia

Mild to moderate hypoglycaemia

- act swiftly

- give rapidly absorbed carbohydrate including one of the following

    — jelly beans (4 large, 7 small)

    — fruit juice (1/2 to 1/3 glass)

    — sugary soft drink

    — glucose tablets equivalent to 10–15 grams

    — sugar, honey, sweetened condensed milk or jam (2–3 teaspoons)

Repeat this treatment if there has been no response within 10–15 minutes

- Follow up by giving slow absorbing carbohydrates, ie bread or starchy biscuits.

- Supervise — never leave the person alone. Intake of appropriate food or drink is required until the person has fully recovered. If the symptoms improve the person may return to the activity after 15 minutes.

- Notify the parents or guardian or carer — do not allow the child to go home unaccompanied.

Severe hypoglycaemia

- Lie the person in the recovery position to avoid them hurting themselves.

- Perform usual first aid — airways, breathing and circulation.

- You may need to give the person some glucagon. This is a hormone that raises the blood glucose levels within 10 minutes. Only appropriately trained people should inject glucagon into a child suffering from a hypo. Sugary drinks should be given immediately after this injection, to avoid a relapse into a hypo state.

4.10 Down syndrome

Down syndrome is the most common cause of intellectual disability. It is not a disease or an illness. The primary cause is one of the unsolved mysteries of genetics, although the mechanism by which it happens is well understood. The syndrome has many characteristic features which can be exhibited individually in many variable forms (Jobling 1991).

Potential problems associated with Down syndrome

No one person with Down syndrome will have all the features listed here. It is usual for a person with Down syndrome to have six or seven of the 125 features that have been identified with Down syndrome. With the exception of some degree of intellectual disability there is no one feature that is present in all individuals with Down syndrome.

Upper respiratory infections

This is the most common medical problem associated with Down syndrome. Some children, particularly in early childhood, can have upper respiratory infections for up to 80% of the year. This will affect the child's hearing, attention, concentration, stamina and attendance.

Heart problems

Up to half the people with Down syndrome are born with some form of heart defect. Heart problems are the single most common form of mortality in infants with Down syndrome. These defects are normally treated surgically or through medication, often with great success.

Skeletal problems

The most common skeletal condition in Down syndrome is atlantoaxial instability (12–20%). This is a genetic condition that results in the misalignment of the cervical vertebrae C1 and C2. People with atlantoaxial instability can display muscle weakness, difficulty in walking, neck discomfort and limited neck mobility. There may also be joint laxity in other areas of the body, and this can cause dislocation or other orthopaedic conditions. While these are not as common as atlantoaxial instability they may restrict certain movement patterns.

Hypotonia

Hypotonia has been described as an increase in the range of motion of the joints, diminished resistance of the joints to passive movements and unusual postures such as the frog-like position of the legs in the supine position (Dubowitz 1980).

There is no known cause for hypotonia although it is a common condition associated with Down syndrome. Low muscle tone and joint laxity may improve as the child gets older although they often persist into adulthood.

Obesity

There is a propensity for people with Down syndrome to be overweight. This may be due to a combination of inactivity and diet (see also 4.17, 'Obesity').

Vision problems

It is common for people with Down syndrome to have vision problems such as cataracts, strabismus (cross-eyes), nystagmus and myopia. A cataract is a cloudiness of the lens that interferes with light transmission to the retina. Strabismus is caused by a muscle imbalance in the eye causing visual acuity problems. Nystagmus refers to the rapid back-and-forth movement of the eye in response to visual stimulus. People with Down syndrome often have protracted nystagmus, meaning the eye overreacts to normal visual stimulus. Myopia (short sightedness) is reported in up to 80% of people with Down syndrome (O'Dell 1988).

Hearing problems

Hearing loss and ear infections are common in people with Down syndrome. The inability to locate sounds and to distinguish between two sounds may also be a problem. Hearing aids and speech therapy are often used.

Kinaesthetic problems

The inability to process information regarding the body and objects in space has also been reported to be a common problem in people with Down syndrome (Schmidt 1988). Some people with Down syndrome may have problems discriminating between different objects according to texture, size and weight.

Problems in timing

Anticipation and timing among people with Down syndrome may be a problem. While this may improve with practice, individuals may differ markedly in their ability to initiate appropriate movements to some external event.

Behaviour

Many children with Down syndrome are often described as stubborn. This is often due to the child not being able to understand the language used, too high/low expectations, failure avoidance and/or sensory overload such as too much noise or activity.

Implications for physical activity

- Consult the person's physician before beginning any program. This is particularly important for young people with Down syndrome since there may be activities that endanger him/her.

- Whilst existence of a particular condition, such as atlantoaxial instability, should not necessarily preclude an individual from participation, it may mean modifying the activity (eg water starts instead of dive starts in swimming).

- Activities that place an undue stress on the head and neck — certain gymnastic activities, heading a soccer ball, high jump — should be avoided or alternatives found if atlantoaxial instability is present.

- Similarly, where a severe heart defect is present, overexertion or sudden bouts of effort should be avoided.

- Balance and strength activities are particularly useful for people with Down syndrome especially during early formative years. These will help counteract stability and muscle tone problems later in life.

- It may be that the person with Down syndrome does not understand the concept of danger. Consider using a buddy system to ensure that safety precautions are taken during activity.

- People with intellectual disabilities learn more effectively when skills are broken down into small achievable targets. Set routines for learning, use visual and/or auditory cues, equipment markers and stop and start signals. See some of the behaviour management techniques outlined under 4.4 (Autism) — many are applicable to all people with intellectual disabilities.

- Many people with Down syndrome appear to have a very high pain threshold. It is not unusual for serious injuries to go unnoticed until severe swelling occurs and/or behaviour changes. Ensure that all injuries are investigated and reported to carers.

- Most people with Down syndrome will have better receptive language than expressive language. When giving instructions keep these to a two-stage command, and use simple language. It is helpful to emphasise key words.

4.11   Emotional disturbances

Like Attention Deficit Hyperactivity Disorder, 'emotional disturbances' have been categorised under a number of headings. People with emotional disturbances may be described as emotionally disordered, behaviourally disabled, emotionally handicapped, mentally ill or psychologically disturbed. Since emotional disturbances can cover distinct characteristics associated with personality, substance abuse or schizophrenic disorders, it is more beneficial to examine the general characteristics of emotional disturbances rather than any precise definitions.

Recognising emotional disturbances

Generally, a young person who is emotionally disturbed exhibits one or more of the following characteristics over a long period of time (usually at least six months).

- an inability to learn at the expected developmentally appropriate rate

- an inability to build and maintain interpersonal relationships with peers and teachers the young person may behave in antisocial or asocial ways which adversely affect their relationships with others

- inappropriate reactions to the environment, causing unexplained withdrawal or aggressive behaviour toward activity

- a general mood of unhappiness

- the development of fears or anxieties associated with perceived personal or school problems.

There are many signs of emotional disturbance. Again, consult parents and professionals to ascertain the individual characteristics and needs of the young person. Do not be too hasty to label an individual as emotionally disturbed.

Implications for physical activity

- Behaviourally/emotionally disturbed people are an extremely heterogeneous population with many varying traits. It is essential to individualise your program for these people.

- The general objectives of a physical activity program for emotionally disturbed people are the same as for those without disabilities.

- The program should emphasise the development of motor skills, physical fitness, social skills and personal development.

- Be aware of any medication being taken and its effect on the individual (often sedatives, anticonvulsants and neuroleptics are prescribed).

- Where appropriate, use regular strong prompts to gain attention, including tactile stimulation.

- Remove distractions and other pieces of equipment lying around.

- Use manual guidance where appropriate. Build up a rapport with the individual and keep in mind that manual manipulation is generally more successful with people who are withdrawn than with those who are hyperactive.

- Encourage responsible behaviour and when necessary impose limits on conduct and on the use of equipment and facilities.

- Do not overdo the desire for control in all situations. Achieving obedience to authority does not facilitate adequate social adjustment for people with emotional disturbances. The individual should learn to independently adjust to various situations.

- Discourage inappropriate interaction. Disruptive behaviour may sometimes mean separating some young people from the group. Try to identify particular disruptive behaviour that can be controlled. Certain behaviour may be triggered by the environment, the activity or certain actions within the group. You may be able to control or eliminate some of these.

- Promote and reward success. Activities that demonstrate immediate positive feedback (eg hitting a ball, striking a target) help motivate the individual to continue and develop skills.

4.12 Epilepsy

Epilepsy is having recurrent seizures or fits. A seizure or fit is caused by a sudden increase in electrochemical activity in the brain. The part of the brain in which this activity occurs determines the visible manifestation of the seizure.

Essentially there are two internationally recognised classifications of seizures:

Partial seizures — where seizure activity originates in one half of the brain or focal point.

Generalised seizures — where seizure activity involves the whole brain. Sometimes a seizure starts as a partial seizure and then progresses to a generalised seizure. When this occurs the seizure is identified as secondary generalised.

Types of epileptic seizures

There are several types of seizures, and they can vary between either a convulsive or non-convulsive. The most common types of seizures include:

- tonic-clonic
- absence
- simple partial
- complex partial

Convulsive including tonic-clonic seizures

generalised tonic-clonic seizures

Generalised tonic-clonic seizures involve the whole brain either from the outset or after spreading from the focal area in the brain. There is a loss of consciousness, the body stiffens and limbs jerk. These seizures generally last one to three minutes after which the person may wish to rest or sleep. They may have a headache or be confused or disorientated.

Non-convulsive which includes absence, simple partial and complex partial seizures

absence seizures

Absence seizures mostly affect children. These seizures also involve the whole brain and are associated with brief (up to 30 seconds) periods of loss of consciousness that may occur many times a day. There is no loss of muscle tone. Absence seizures are often mistaken for daydreaming or lack of concentration and can disrupt learning by creating gaps in information received.

partial seizures

Partial seizures are so called because they originate in one cerebral hemisphere and only affect that part of the brain — not because they are part of a seizure.

Simple partial seizures effect a change to motor function or sensation. The person may experience a stiffening or jerking of a limb, strange feelings in the stomach, or an alteration of taste or smell. Consciousness is not impaired. Auras are simple partial seizures and vary greatly in experience. An aura can precede a complex partial seizure or a tonic-clonic seizure. Where it precedes a tonic-clonic seizure the aura can act as a warning, giving the person time to seek a safe place before losing consciousness.

Complex partial seizures differ from simple partial seizures in that there is some alteration to consciousness. These seizures can vary widely depending on the part of the brain involved and they generally last only a few minutes. The person may experience a stiffening or jerking of part of the body and may be unresponsive and confused, repeatedly picking at clothing or hair. Purposeless actions such as lip-smacking or chewing may occur along with temporary speech impairment.

Most people with epilepsy have their seizures controlled by anti-epileptic medication.

Implications for physical activity

- Discuss with parent/s, carer or guardian the individual's particular epilepsy syndrome, seizure type/s and frequency, and medication requirements.

- Familiarise yourself with the appropriate first aid response to seizures.

- In the event of a seizure note what the person was doing before the seizure, what the person did during the seizure, how long the active phase lasted, and how long before the person was responsive.

- If the student's seizures are not fully controlled by medication, educate the class about epilepsy generally and what to do in case of a seizure. A seizure can be a frightening experience for all and the class will be better prepared if a seizure occurs.

- If seizures are largely controlled through medication, people with epilepsy can participate in nearly all forms of physical activity. Consult with parent/s, carer or guardian to establish what limits, if any, are necessary.

- If seizures are not fully controlled by medication, close one-to-one supervision is required especially around water.

- Good practice for water sports such as swimming, canoeing, sailing and snorkeling is the utilisation of the buddy system, as well as a lifeguard and/or lifejacket.

- Be aware that sports such as boxing, mountain/rock climbing and scuba diving may cause specific problems for people with epilepsy.

- Physical exhaustion can trigger seizures — monitor the individual closely after long periods of exertion and if possible avoid situations where the individual becomes distressed.

- Seizures can occur during the cool-down period after exercise. Again, monitor this period carefully.

- Common seizure triggers are missed medication, use of alcohol, lack of sleep, stress and menstruation.

SEIZURE FIRST AID — WHAT TO DO

- Stay calm
- Time the seizure
- Do not try to restrain the person
- Do not put anything in their mouth
- Do not apply CPR
- Protect the person from obvious injury
- Clear the area of harmful objects
- Loosen tie or collar
- Place something soft under head and shoulders
- As soon as possible roll the person onto their side and keep the airway clear
- Stay with and reassure the person until they have fully recovered

If a seizure occurs in water

- Hold the person's head above the water
- Stay with the person and call for help
- Assist the person from the water when the seizure is over

If a seizure occurs in a wheelchair

- Do not try to remove the person from this position
- Ensure that the wheelchair is secure
- Protect the person from falling if they are not restrained
- Protect the person by gently supporting their head
- Assist the person from the wheelchair when the seizure is over if the airway is blocked
- Stay with and reassure the person until they have fully recovered

Call an ambulance if

- the active or jerking movements of the seizure last for more than five minutes or longer than normal for that person
- another seizure quickly follows
- the person has been injured
- you are in doubt.

4.13 HIV/AIDS and blood disorders

HIV (Human Immunodeficiency Virus) is the virus that causes AIDS (Acquired Immune Deficiency Syndrome). HIV damages the immune system, which causes the body to become less able to protect itself from disease and illness. Without treatment, HIV graduates to AIDS, and opportunist diseases which eventually lead to the death of people who are HIV positive.

The underlying pathology of HIV and AIDS is the fact that there is immune deficiency. Different people will be affected differently by HIV and AIDS related diseases because of the different areas in which they live and the unique situations they experience.

Haemophilia

Haemophilia is a rare blood clotting disorder in which one of the blood clotting factors is deficient. It is caused by an inherited gene, and affects males almost exclusively. The general belief about haemophilia — that haemophiliacs tend to bleed excessively and bleed to death rapidly — is false. People with haemophilia bleed at the same rate as everyone else, they just bleed for longer.

Hepatitis B and C

Hepatitis is a disease that causes inflammation of the liver. It can be passed through blood and other bodily fluids, usually through contact with an open wound or the inside lining of the body.

Preventing the spread of HIV/AIDS and blood disorders

- Carers should wear gloves, and clean blood spills with a paper towel, followed by a soapy water wash. If there is a possibility that the carer has had skin contact with the blood, ensure that household strength bleach is used to wash the area.

- Don't share items such as toothbrushes, razors or nail-clippers with people with a blood infection.

- Any items that have blood on them should be placed in a leak-proof bag before being discarded.

Implications for physical activity

- Exercise and physical activity is a good way of enhancing well-being and maintaining good health. Regular exercise to maintain body weight and in particular muscle tissue may help prevent damage to the immune system and help slow disease progression.

- It is important to get a medical check and dietary advice for people with HIV/AIDS before starting any physical activity or sport program.

- Ensure that care is taken when people with HIV/AIDS are participating in contact or combat sports.

- If a person with HIV/AIDS has a wound do not let them participate in sport until the wound has healed. Similarly, if a person sustains a bleeding wound while playing sport, treat it immediately. Cover the wound with a waterproof dressing and once again allow the wound to completely heal before the commencement of physical activity.

- Try to ensure that the activity does not place too much stress on a person. Above-normal exertion can put the person's immune system under further stress.

- Sports such as cycling, swimming and jogging that are low in intensity and increase endurance are beneficial for people with HIV/AIDS. Also of benefit are low intensity weight programs that help to build and tone muscle.

- Be aware of the fact that as AIDS progresses, vision may become impaired. Ensure that you modify physical activity to accommodate the changing needs and abilities of the person.

4.14 Juvenile rheumatoid arthritis and osteoporosis

Juvenile rheumatoid arthritis (JRA) is a general term used to describe arthritis in children. The term arthritis means 'inflammation of a joint' and refers to more than 150 different rheumatic conditions (Goodman 1993). The common characteristic of juvenile arthritis is the inflammation of the lining of one or more joints. JRA usually occurs in children at about six years of age. It affects more girls than boys, is progressive and has no known cause. Children with arthritis should be encouraged to participate in sport and physical activity. Activities such as swimming and cycling promote a sense of well-being as well as increasing strength that supports bones and joints affected by the disease.

The onset of chronic or severe arthritis may affect other areas of the child's development, including:

- growth — inflammation may slow the child's growth, which should return to normal once the arthritis has improved.

- eye problems — occasionally inflammation inside the eye may accompany arthritis.

Arthritis is unpredictable. It may affect a child for several months and then disappear; in other children the arthritis becomes chronic and the children experience constant flare-ups throughout their lives. The individual will require frequent rest periods and physical therapy during these periods. The disease may go into remission for periods although periods of acute illness may recur at any time.

Symptoms of juvenile rheumatoid arthritis

The common characteristic of JRA is the inflammation of the lining of one or more joints. It is currently believed that this inflammation is caused by the body's own immune system, but the reason for this inflammation is unknown. The immune system may think it has identified an infection in the body and — as a result of fighting the infection — cause prolonged inflammation, resulting in JRA.

The affected joints of a child with arthritis

- are typically swollen and warm to touch;

- may have a pinkish rash over the affected joints;

- are limited in their range of motion, and

- are stiff and painful.

There is no known cause of arthritis, but we know that the disease is not hereditary, that is it cannot be passed on from parent to child, and that a family history of the disease does not make a child more susceptible.

Osteoporosis

Osteoporosis is a condition in which the bones become more porous and thus more fragile and prone to injuries such as fractures. There is no cure for osteoporosis, but there are preventative measures.

It is important that preventative steps are initiated from an early age, thus reducing the chance of developing the disease. Up to 80% of bone composition is determined by genetics, thus there is nothing we can do to alter the bone makeup. However there are ways we can enhance our genetic potential and maximise the other factors that influence the other 20% of bone development.

Prevention strategies for osteoporosis

- Family history is a strong risk factor in the development of osteoporosis. Maintaining a healthy lifestyle will help offset the development of the disease.

- Exercising while young will help to improve the skeleton. Weight bearing and high impact exercise has been proven to be the most beneficial in the development of a healthy skeleton.

- Eat sufficient amounts of calcium. Inadequate amounts of calcium places extra stress on the skeleton, increasing the chance of injury and deterioration of the skeleton.

- Eating disorders are known to have a negative effect on bone development and maintenance. Because of insufficient nutrients and a lack of oestrogen in the body, a person with an eating disorder may become more prone to developing osteoporosis.

Implications for physical activity

- Check with the person's physician, doctor or occupational therapist whether activities such as jumping, diving and leaping, or frequent falls, are contraindicated during periods of remission.

- Exercise helps prevent the loss of joint movement and promotes normal growth.

- There may be difficulties in performing activities that require gripping or fine motor movements for young people where JRA affects the hand and wrist.

- Because acute illness may mean long periods of rest, physical fitness levels may have deteriorated. Design your program with this in mind; allow for rest periods.

- Aquatic activities are particularly useful; warm water is recommended to relax joints.

- The most beneficial types of exercise for people with arthritis include those that target flexibility, strengthen the muscles and build aerobic fitness.

- The best time for a person with arthritis to exercise is when they are pain-free, not fatigued, and when their medication is working at its most effective.

- Keep in mind that physical activity programs are vital as self-management techniques for arthritis. Some studies report that over-resting is as much a danger to the arthritic person as over-exercise (Lynberg and Danneskiol-Samsoe 1988).

- Gentle exercise and hydrotherapy may help ease some of the pain of arthritis.

- Exercise should stop if the person has a decreased range of motion, increased inflammation of the joints, continued pain, increased weakness or unusual fatigue.

4.15 Mental health

Mental illness is a series of illnesses or conditions — just as heart disease encompasses many diseases that affect the functioning of the heart, mental illness encompasses many conditions. People with a mental illness may experience an episode of the illness only once in their lifetime or they may be subject to relapses over the course of their lives.

Mental illness is either psychotic or non-psychotic.

A **psychosis** is a type of disease which affect the brain, resulting in changes of thoughts, emotions and behaviour. People with a psychosis tend to become isolated from the outside environment. Their perception of what they believe to be real (compared with what is actually real for everyone else) becomes distorted and in fact is not experienced by others at all. People perceive their world very differently.

A **non-psychotic** illness, where the person experiences emotions that are extremely intense, is characterised by the person having trouble coping with everyday experiences such as work, relationships and leisure activities. People with this type of mental illness tend to keep it within themselves. Often, immediate family and peers have no idea that the person is experiencing any emotional difficulty at all.

Understanding mental illness

It is important for people with a mental health issue that those people in their immediate environment understand their illness. Because of the lack of understanding by society in regards to mental health, ignorance, stereotypes and misinformation surround it. This results in isolation and discrimination of the person with a mental illness.

- Mental illness is not a form of intellectual disability or brain damage. Mental illness is just like any other form of illness, physical or otherwise, and the people with the illness should receive the same support and caring that physical illness demands.

- Mental illness is curable. With appropriate treatment, many people with a mental health condition will be able to lead fulfilling lives.

- Anyone can develop a mental illness. Although the cause of mental illness is unknown, triggering factors have been identified, and they include stress.

- People with a mental illness are not dangerous. This is a grave misconception. People who are receiving appropriate treatment are rarely dangerous.

Some common mental illnesses

- eating disorders

- anxiety disorders

- depression

- bipolar mood disorder

Eating disorders

The most commonly recognised types of eating disorders include anorexia and bulimia. Because eating disorders affect mainly teenage girls and women in their early twenties, it is important to develop healthy eating habits and a positive body image early in life. People who have an eating disorder have an obsession with controlling their body weight, food consumption and eating patterns.

- People with anorexia have a desire to control the amount of food they eat.

- People with bulimia often feel out of control about food. There is no consistency in their eating habits, a binge is often followed by purging.

There is no single cause of an eating disorder, but some factors are believed to influence the onset of the illness. Low self-esteem is deemed as a significant contributor. When combined with other social, psychological and biological factors the problem compounds itself, manifesting itself in an eating disorder.

Other health issues are associated with eating disorders — one of these is the development of osteoporosis. Studies have found that there is a link between eating disorders and the development of osteoporosis.

Anxiety disorders

Everyone experiences feelings of anxiety as part of normal everyday happenings (response to fear, danger or stress), but people with an anxiety disorder often have constant feelings of high anxiety. There are feelings of continual or extreme apprehension and tension with the fear of panic attacks; the cause or source of these feelings is usually unknown. When these feelings become so intense that normal daily function is hindered or stopped, a person is diagnosed as having an anxiety disorder.

Anxiety disorders can affect the way a person thinks, feels and behaves, and if they are not treated can cause considerable distress.

The causes of anxiety disorders may not be obvious in every case, and often the causes vary. There are factors that have been associated with the development of anxiety disorders. People who are easily aroused or upset, or who are extremely sensitive, may be more prone to developing an anxiety disorder. Heightened anxiety may become a learnt response when faced with particular situations, or a child may learn the response from their parents or family.

Types of anxiety disorders

- Separation Anxiety Disorder — is characterised by excessive anxiety when separated from the parent or primary carer.

- Specific Phobia — a child with this anxiety disorder has an intense, persistent and unrealistic fear of an identifiable situation or object. This is common among children and treatment is not required unless it interferes with the child's functioning.

- Panic Disorder — the person has panic attacks and sudden overwhelming sense of fear in situations where most people would not be afraid. Is often accompanied by agoraphobia.

- Agoraphobia — people with this disorder fear being in a situation or a place where they feel out of control, where they may become embarrassed or which they may not be able to get away from.

- Generalised Anxiety Disorder — involves prolonged worry about life practices and the possibility of catastrophic occurrences as a result.

- Obsessive Compulsive Disorder — a person with this disorder is plagued with unwanted thoughts, and often repeats specific actions in an attempt to rid themselves of the thoughts.

- Tourette's Syndrome — is characterised by repetitive involuntary muscle movements and/or vocalisations.

Depression

Depression is a term given to a series of illnesses characterised by extended periods of sadness or a depressed mood, which affects a person's life. People with depression may appear constantly sad. They may no longer enjoy regular activities and may feel irritable and anxious. They may experience periods of extreme boredom and lethargy and their eating habits could alter.

Depression can occur in people when they are faced with difficult circumstances they are ill equipped to deal with. Divorce, poverty, illness and abuse are just a few situations that may affect a person's mental state. People without these major strains can also suffer depression.

As with other forms of mental illness, the cause of depression may vary between people. Factors that can be relevant in the development of depression include personality type, stress, heredity, and biochemical imbalance; in some cases it may be a learnt response.

Types of depression
- Adjustment Disorder with Depressed Mood — depression may result as a greater reaction than normal to a distressing situation in a person's life. People with this disorder usually experience feelings of anxiousness, have disrupted sleep patterns and may lose their appetite.

- Depressive episodes — these are perhaps the most severe form of depression. They are believed to be the result of a chemical imbalance in the brain. This illness can affect all people, even those in happy, well-adjusted lives. In the most serious cases of depressive episode, a psychotic depression is developed. A person with psychotic depression may lose touch with reality and start to hear voices telling them that they are worthless, wicked and deserve to be punished.

Bipolar mood disorder

This is a disorder in which the person experiences extreme mood swings, from extreme depression to elation and excitement. Some people experience only attacks of mania without the feelings of despair.

Symptoms of bipolar mood disorder
- mania: elevated mood — the person is extremely high, happy and full of energy

  irritability — the person gets upset with people who disagree with them

  rapid thinking and speech

  lack of inhibitions

  grandiose plans and beliefs

  lack of insight

- depression — many people who experience bipolar mood disorder suffer from periods of depression, which may be triggered by stress or traumatic event in their lives.

- normal moods — in between the bouts of mania or depression, people with bipolar mood disorder have relatively regular lives, they are able to function as any other person would.

The causes of bipolar mood disorder are similar to other causes of mental illness. With genetic and biochemical factors influencing mood type, stress and seasons also affect the person's mood state. If left untreated, bipolar disorder can lead to bouts of mania or clinical depression.

Implications for physical activity

- Bring mental illness into the open. Treat it as you would any physical illness or disability. Remember to respect confidentiality if this is an issue.

- Educate other people about the condition. Help them overcome the stigma associated with mental illness.

- Include the person with a mental illness in all sports or physical activities, unless told otherwise by the parent or doctor.

- Be aware that physical activity and sport, for example competitive team sports and certain coaching/teaching styles, can induce stress and anxiety and aggravate particular conditions.

- For people with eating disorders be aware of the possible effects of high energy activities and monitor an individual's energy states and eating habits before and after exercise.

- As a coach/teacher of a person with a mental illness, particularly depression and bipolar mood disorder, stay calm, emphasise the positive aspects of participation, and encourage the individual to have fun and enjoy the experience.

- Research studies have shown that people with bipolar mood disorder and depression react positively to physical activity.

- Very few medications have implications for physical activity. However, make yourself aware of any possible ramifications.

4.16 Muscular dystrophy

Muscular dystrophy is considered as a group of inherited diseases that are characterised by progressive, diffuse weakness of various muscle groups. The dystrophy itself is not fatal, but secondary complications of muscle weakness predispose the person to respiratory disorders and heart problems. It is quite common for dystrophic individuals in advanced stages of the disease to die from a simple respiratory infection. The specific causes of muscular dystrophies remain unknown (Winnick 1990).

Types of dystrophies and other major muscle disorders

Here, we will consider only the four main types of muscular dystrophy. The most severe type of muscular dystrophy is *Duchenne* type. This mainly affects males, many of whom do not reach adulthood.

Duchenne (or Progressive) muscular dystrophy

In young children, usually about 5–6 years, Duchenne muscular dystrophy is characterised by difficulties in standing up, climbing stairs, a tendency to fall and a waddling gait. Progression of the disease can lead to the individual being unable to walk within 10 years. 'Pseudo hypertrophy' is a characteristic of Duchenne muscular dystrophy. This means that a false appearance of muscle development may occur, particularly in the calf and forearm muscles, as an excessive build up of adipose and connective tissues give the mistaken impression of healthy musculature.

As the disease progresses the functional ability of the individual regresses to the point where he/she requires an electric wheelchair for ambulation. Fortunately, degeneration of the hand and finger muscles does not occur at the same rate as other muscle groups and the individual is able to operate an electric wheelchair as long as he/she is able to remain in a sitting position.

Facio-scapulo-humeral muscular dystrophy

This is the second most common type of muscular dystrophy. Males and females are equally likely to contract the disease. It affects the shoulder and upper arm and also results in a weakening of the face muscles. This may result in an expressionless appearance. Later, weakness may also appear in the hip, pelvic and abdominal muscle groups. This weakening process often leads to lordosis and/or scoliosis (poor posture). Facio-scapulo-humeral muscular dystrophy is not as severe as Duchenne type and people are often able to live long and productive lives.

Limb girdle muscular dystrophy

Weakness in the shoulder girdle muscles or the hip and thigh muscles usually occurs in teenage years. Early symptoms include difficulty in raising arms above shoulder height or awkwardness in climbing stairs. While muscle degeneration progresses slowly, eventually the upper and lower extremities may be affected.

Myotonic muscular dystrophy

This usually occurs in early adulthood and results in progressive muscle weakness. Characteristics include a 'hatchet face' appearance, frontal balding and behavioural and psychiatric childhood problems (Sherrill 1993). Myotonic muscular dystrophy results in an inability to rapidly relax muscles following a sustained voluntary contraction (eg closing the eyelids tightly or shaking hands).

Implications for physical activity

- Physical activity significantly enhances the quality of life for people with muscular dystrophy.

- Physical activity also plays an important role in managing muscular dystrophy — in particular, breathing games and stretching exercises are important once the individual is permanently in a wheelchair. Inactivity can contribute to muscle degeneration.

- For those with a less severe condition, muscle strengthening and range of motion exercises are important to help the individual remain mobile for as long as possible.

- Remember that a person with muscular dystrophy is likely to tire easily because of muscle weakness. Pace your activities so that the individual gets the most out of the activity without over-tiring him/her excessively.

- Aquatic activities are particularly beneficial, aid muscle tone and flexibility, and encourage circulation.

- Developing good relaxation techniques can be extremely important for the person with muscular dystrophy as the progressive loss of functional skills gradually increases stress.

- Try and develop skills that will be of use later in life. Take into consideration the degenerative nature of the disease.

  For example, a child with Duchenne muscular dystrophy could be taught to play bocce — a game that can easily be played with limited muscle involvement.

4.17 Obesity

People whose weight is more than 20% over their desired body weight according to a growth chart are generally considered obese. This is very much an arbitrary figure, however, and should be taken as the 'cut off' point between people who are overweight and those who are not.

Obesity is now recognised as a serious problem among school aged children. The problems of obesity are as much 'mental' as physical. If obesity occurs in early childhood the chances of adult obesity are three times greater. It restricts functional ability and is a major risk factor for a number of health related conditions, including cardiovascular disease, diabetes, renal disease, osteoarthritis and several types of cancer. It is essential that we do not ignore the fact that the main concern for people who are obese is the obesity-induced medical problems (immediate or potential).

Causes of obesity

Obesity and 'overweightness' can have many causes. An individual may have a genetic predisposition to obesity, particularly if both parents are overweight. Caloric imbalance, eating incorrectly in relation to energy expenditure, can be a factor. Dysfunction of the endocrine glands (the pituitary and thyroid) can cause the overproduction of fat cells. Sedentary lifestyles, particularly in the age of computer games and television, can be another major cause of childhood obesity.

Implications for physical activity

- Teach children that it is normal for young people to have various body shapes and sizes. There is considerable social pressure to conform to certain body types — while your program will undoubtedly help counteract obesity, do not stress this as a major purpose of exercise.

- There is considerable evidence to suggest that obesity can cause undesirable emotional and social characteristics. Try to create a program that is geared to success for the individual. This will help build confidence and self-esteem.

- Be aware that some obese individuals can experience discomfort during physical activity, such as chafing between thighs and other skin areas, bobbing up and down of abdomen and breasts, retention of fluids causing swelling in ankles and wrists, and certain postural defects that affect the efficiency of movements.

- Do not exclude people from activities because of their size.

- Your program may be a part of a total weight management program for the obese individual. This may include counselling, diet and drug control measures. Liaise with the appropriate people so that all parts of the 'total' program are working together.

- Consider developing a behaviour management program for young people who are obese (see pages 199–200 of Horvat 1990 for examples of appropriate weight loss and behaviour management techniques for obese individuals).

4.18 Schizophrenia

Schizophrenia is a term given to a group of psychoses in which deterioration of functioning is marked by severe distortion of thought perception and mood, bizarre behaviour and social withdrawal. Not all people with schizophrenia exhibit all these symptoms. It affects one in every one hundred Australians, and during the onset of the disease the person may experience withdrawal from others, be depressed and anxious, and develop fears and obsessions.

Major symptoms of schizophrenia

Delusions

Delusions are firmly held beliefs that have no basis in reality. Even when confronted with contradictory evidence, a delusional person fails to believe otherwise. Most delusions can be categorised as:

— delusions of persecution

— delusions of control (thought broadcasting, thought withdrawal)

— delusions of reference (believe their lives are being depicted in public)

— delusions of sin and guilt (claim to have hurt someone, stealing)

— hypochondria/psychosomatic delusions

— nihilistic delusions (think the world has ceased to exist)

— delusions of grandeur (believe they are famous or powerful)

Hallucinations

People who have hallucinations often hear voices. Other people may experience a false belief that they are sensing (ie tasting, seeing, feeling or smelling) something that is real, when it is not actually there.

Disorganised speech

A person with schizophrenia may lose their ability to articulate their thoughts and feelings. The frequency and duration of speech may be reduced, and often inappropriate responses to external situations occur.

Disorganised or catatonic behaviour

Catatonic behaviour involves a person being hindered in their movement. They may have a dull and expressionless appearance. The other extreme sees a person exhibiting unexplained behaviour and disorganised thinking.

Negative symptoms

When normal functions such as speech and behaviour are reduced, a person is experiencing negative symptoms of schizophrenia.

- Other symptoms of schizophrenia include a loss of drive or motivation — they may withdraw from social occasions because of reduced social skills, and a schizophrenic person may be oblivious to other conditions and ailments they are experiencing.

Types of schizophrenic disorders

There are a number of what are known as *schizophrenic disorders*. These include disordered type, catatonic type, paranoid type, undifferentiated type and residual type.

Disordered type

People with a disordered type of schizophrenia are generally very poor at associating meaning to their physical world. They display erratic and incoherent modes of behaviour that are inappropriate to their surroundings. The child may assume erratic postures, giggle uncontrollably, pull faces, have incoherent speech, and mood disturbance.

Catatonic type

People with a catatonic type of schizophrenia often have one persistent mode of behaviour that characterises their everyday reactions to external stimulus. This may mean a marked decrease in reactivity to environmental stimulus and/or a reduction in spontaneous movements (catatonic stupor); an apparent resistance to any forms of instruction (catatonic negativism); a physical resistance to movement (catatonic rigidity); an unexplainable excited physical outburst (catatonic excitement) or voluntary inappropriate posturing (catatonic posturing).

Paranoid type

This type of schizophrenia is characterised by delusions and hallucinations. The hallucinations are relatively consistent in nature, usually with underlying themes of grandeur, persecution or conspiracy.

Undifferentiated type

In this type of schizophrenia there are prominent delusions, hallucinations, incoherence or disorganised behaviour.

Residual type

This type is characterised by a general evidence of disturbance without prominent undifferentiated type of schizophrenia.

Implications for physical activity

- Sherrill (1993) identifies four general principles for working with people with schizophrenia. These include:

    1. Graded reversal of deterioration

       This involves building on an individual's appropriate behaviour while not necessarily taking away completely all inappropriate behaviour. The person must not feel disapproval at his/her actions, but rather, only approval of appropriate reactions.

    2. Constructive progress

       Meaning the gradual introduction of age appropriate modes of behaviour. People often display a reluctance to 'grow up'; introducing and applauding more mature behaviour helps promote more age appropriate behaviour.

    3. Education toward reality

       Instead of appearing interested in or somehow encouraging 'fantasy' type behaviour, the 'education toward reality' principle means continually reminding the young person about reality. Recommended responses to hallucinations are 'you know that is not true' or 'that doesn't make sense.'

    4. Directive guidance

       This involves educating the young person about the difference between right and wrong. People with schizophrenia may need telling what others learn naturally or pick up along the way. This includes recognising authority (umpires and referees) and understanding game structures and rules.

- People with schizophrenia can display quite aggressive reactions to criticism and/or negative stimulus. Hostility is basically a protective reaction and should not always be met with anger, particularly with young people with schizophrenia.

- As a rule, avoid conflict that may cause temper tantrums. If the young person becomes aggressive, try and introduce a new toy or game as a distraction. Try to remain calm and not show anger or fear about a particular behaviour. Do not use punishment — this tends to reinforce paranoid beliefs.

- Reward appropriate and 'good' behaviour.

- Structure play groups/team games so that aggressive people are not in direct 'conflict'.

- Ensure that you are aware of any medication being taken (how often, how much?). Schizophrenic people on medication may slow down, lose their appetite and experience sleeplessness. Medications for these conditions might also affect balance and coordination.

(**4.19**) Spina bifida

Spina bifida is the most common congenital defect of the spine. Spina bifida is a developmental defect of the spinal column in which vertebral arches have failed to fuse posteriorly in part of the spine. The underlying spinal cord also fails to complete its development thus resulting in spinal cord dysfunction.

Types of spina bifida

There are three types of spina bifida:

1. Myelomeningocele (MM)

This is the most common form of spina bifida, frequently resulting in problems with mobility, toileting and learning. Most children with MM have associated hydrocephalus.

2. Meningocele

This type of spina bifida involves the bones and coverings of the spinal cord, but the spinal cord is usually normal. Therefore, there is no disability. This is the least common form of spina bifida.

3. Spina Bifida Occulta

This is the hidden or closed form of spina bifida that may occasionally result in mobility or toileting problems. Some 5–10% of the population have this condition, but they have no form of disability as a result of this condition.

Myelomeningocele

People with this type of spina bifida may have problems with mobility, toileting and learning. Most will require a shunt for hydrocephalus. Many children will require shoe inserts (orthoses) and a walking frame or crutches for walking. A manual wheelchair will be used by these people as an important means of keeping up with their peer group.

People with mobility problems also have less sensation in their legs and are therefore more prone to damage their skin. Possible causes of such damage are burns from hot concrete or play equipment or heaters, pressure areas on their feet if orthoses or shoes are rubbing, or pressure areas on their buttocks from spending long hours in their wheelchairs. These children are also more prone to fractures as their bones are not as strong. The fracture may not be painful but the leg will be swollen and hot.

Hidden problems of hydrocephalus

Hydrocephalus results from the build-up of fluid within the brain. The surgical treatment for this is a shunt. A shunt is a silastic tube with a pressure valve, which redirects the fluid to another body compartment, usually the abdomen. The valve of the shunt and the tubing can be felt under the skin, just behind the right ear (or sometimes the left) with the tubing passing over the anterior chest wall and into the abdomen. Implanting a shunt controls the build-up of pressure by draining excess cerebrospinal fluid and preventing any additional damage. However, this does not 'cure' the hydrocephalus, and damage to the brain tissue remains.

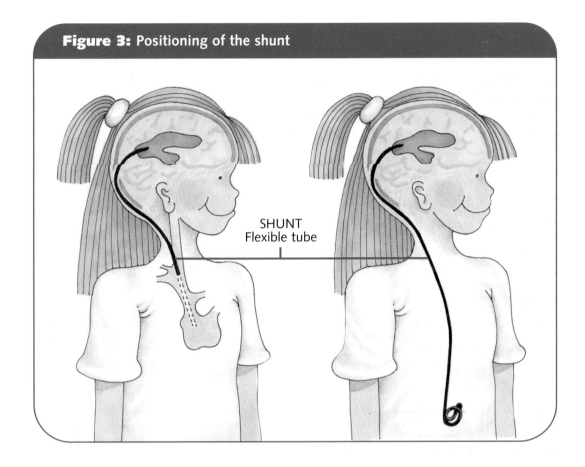

Figure 3: Positioning of the shunt

SHUNT
Flexible tube

People with hydrocephalus frequently have some difficulty learning despite presenting as very social children with good expressive language.

Many children who have spina bifida and/or hydrocephalus have characteristics which only become apparent over time (ie they are not apparent during initial interactions). These are not always recognised as being part of the condition. The following tasks are commonly a problem for people with spina bifida:

- complex instructions

- managing more than one task at a time

- completing a task within a given time

- organising and planning

- motivation and initiation

- self-monitoring and correction

- memory

- conducting in-depth interaction (some young people will have good general social conversation skills for initial interaction, but will have difficulty with in-depth conversation on a topic)

- recollection (they tell you things that they have already discussed with you before)

- focusing their attention on a task for more than a short period

- writing quickly and neatly

- numeracy skills.

The person may be very good in some areas of learning (such as reading and verbal skills) but have difficulty in others as a direct result of their condition. These problems may be difficult to recognise since they are similar to those experienced by other people. However, because the problem lies within the condition, it will not go away or improve without specific attention and understanding.

Implications for physical activity

- People with spina bifida should be encouraged to be as physically active as possible to maintain fitness, prevent obesity and promote participation.

- It is important to identify the position of the shunt and to take care not to displace it when lifting or transferring a person with MM (position hands and arms away from the position of the shunt or tube).

- A shunt can become clogged or malfunction. If this happens it must be replaced. Look for symptoms: headaches, vomiting, lethargy, irritability, swelling and redness along the shunt tract, or changes in personality and behaviour. Clogging or malfunction can also result in seizures.

- Wearing shunts can affect the range of motion in certain throwing activities, and participation in certain activities such as contact sports, 'heading' activities, rolling activities, and diving from heights.

- Progressive strength exercises for upper extremities are important and can easily be incorporated into programs.

- Ensure appropriate protection (eg stockings, or shoes and socks) to a person's legs if the person has poor sensation.

- If there is no sensation in the injured area, watch out for injury to the skin from burns or scrapes. Pressure sores may also develop. People with paralysis may be unaware of the position of their legs, which in turn may place them in hazardous situations.

- Some people with spina bifida might not be able to control the 'blink reflex' — they might shut their eyes as a ball travels towards them.

- While braces may enhance participation in some activities, they may also slow movement. Consider whether standing or sitting is best for any particular activity.

- Make sure that people in wheelchairs have seatbelts so they do not fall out during gross motor activities.

- Swimming is an excellent sport and leisure activity for people with spina bifida.

4.20 Spinal cord injuries

The term spinal cord injury (SCI) usually refers to people who acquire a disability as a result of an accident (trauma or illness) in which the spinal cord is damaged. The severity of an individual's loss of function is determined by many factors. Generally SCI involves the partial or complete loss of motor function, sensory feedback, voluntary bowel and bladder control, impaired circulation, and sometimes impaired function of the internal organs below the site of the injury (Goodman et al 1996).

Types of SCI

It is important to know which area of the spinal cord is damaged, as this determines the level of functional ability. Figure 4 (below) shows spinal cord segments from the first cervical vertebra (C1) to the lowest sacral segment (S4); the functional activities pictured at various levels give you an idea of the effect the location of the damage can have on daily living.

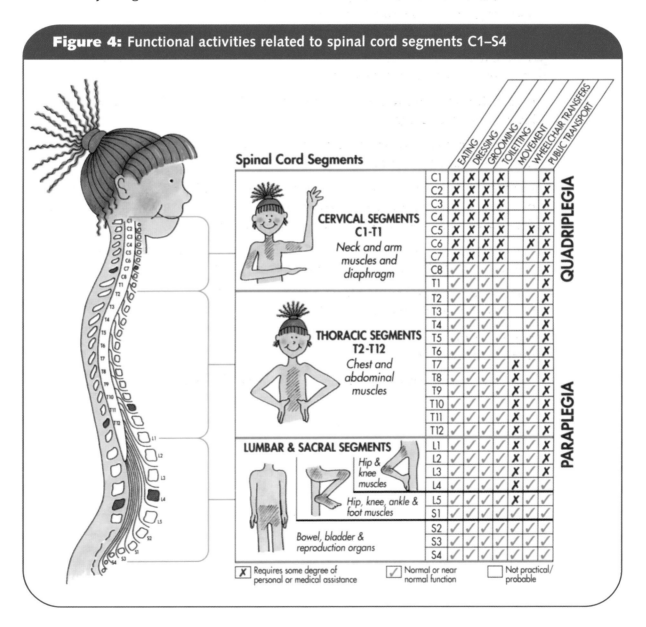

Figure 4: Functional activities related to spinal cord segments C1–S4

There are basically three types of SCI which affect motor function:

1 Paraplegia

A complete or partial loss of function of the trunk and lower limbs. Damage usually occurs lower than quadriplegics, around segment T2 and below.

2 Quadriplegia (or tetraplegia)

Complete or partial loss of function, including movement and/or sensation in the trunk, lower and upper limbs. Damage to the spinal cord is higher in the spinal cord than for paraplegics, around C1–T1.

3 Incomplete lesions

Damage to the spinal cord may be 'incomplete' — meaning the spinal cord is not totally damaged or severed. Some sensation and function may remain below the level of damage.

Implications for physical activity

- Generally speaking, people with SCIs will not have any different learning characteristic than their able-bodied peers. However, the physical impairment may restrict movement, proprioception and the rate of learning.

- Make sure the individual does not have any associated health related conditions that may affect participation in some activities.

- Activities that promote upper body strength and flexibility are important and easily incorporated into regular activities. Basic skills such as throwing, running (rolling), catching, striking and agility skills should be worked on. Pushing a wheelchair requires only a limited range of movement — the individual may develop strong but inflexible muscles.

- Lead-up games for people with SCIs, such as using suspended balls, targets or rebound throwing, will aid the development of basic skills that will be useful later for more intricate games and sports.

- Be aware of safety and access issues. Will there be enough room to move freely? Can the individual access all areas to be used easily?

- Be aware that physical fitness levels for paraplegics have been found to be lower than for their able-bodied peers. It may take longer to build up a comparable level of fitness.

- Aquatics and dance activities do not require many modifications and have the benefits of building on strength and flexibility. Teaching principles are very much the same, depending on the extent of muscle function remaining. Fitness can be worked on while being independent of the wheelchair.

- Quadriplegic people may tire quicker than paraplegics and able-bodied people.

- Upper body strength exercises and flexibility are very important for people with quadriplegia.

- Familiarise yourself with the lifting techniques described in Appendix 2. Plan ahead and enlist a helper or buddy who can assist.

4.21 Transplants

There are five types of transplant recipients:

- heart
- lung
- liver
- kidney
- bone marrow

Sport for transplantees has grown rapidly in the last few years. There are national and international competitions for transplant athletes and organisations set up to help people with transplants get actively involved in sporting competition (see Contacts/Help). Most of the implications for participation involve medical issues rather than sporting considerations. For all transplant recipients there are basically three kinds of medication commonly used:

1. medicine that helps your body accept the new organ
2. medicine that protects you from infection
3. medicine that controls the side effects of transplant medicines

Major organs can be damaged through disease or infection. When an organ is irreversibly damaged through disease or infection, then the person is a candidate for a transplant. Kidney transplants are the most common major organ transplant operation. Kidney transplant recipients are heavily dependent on medication. Bone marrow transplants are performed to fight many different types of cancer and disease.

Immunosuppressants are commonly used to prevent the immune system attacking the new organ. These medicines are very important for all transplant recipients but they can have side effects. A number of steroids are used to combat side effects. Most medicines are strong and medical practitioners generally prescribe ones that help fight infections and combat any likelihood of developing cancers, such as cancer of the lymph gland or skin cancers. Common side effects of transplant medication include:

- changes in appearance due to steroid use
- stomach problems
- fluid retention/high blood pressure
- weight gain
- increased blood sugar/diabetes
- problems with bones and muscles
- changes in behaviour
- eye problems
- tremors or shakiness and headaches
- skin rash or acne

The extent of these side effects will vary between individuals, according to their own body systems and medications.

Implications for physical activity

- Always consult the individual and their medical practitioner before any physical activity program. For competition purposes the Australian Transplant Sports Association (see Contacts/Help) has guidelines for eligibility.

- Do not include a person who is waiting for a transplant in a physical activity program without written approval from a medical practitioner.

- Avoid prolonged exposure to the sun and use sunscreen, hats and protective clothing.

- Ensure all cuts and abrasions are treated quickly by appropriate people.

- Be conscious that high impact sport may not be appropriate for some transplant recipients as osteoporosis may be present.

- Low impact, short duration activities are recommended at the beginning of any program, regardless of the fitness level of the individual.

- Encourage and support the individual — a positive attitude toward participation can increase self esteem and quality of life.

4.22 Vision impairment

Vision impairment refers to any condition that interferes with vision, including total blindness. Most people with vision impairment retain some useful vision. The reason that not all people with vision impairment experience the same dysfunction is that there are numerous ways that vision is damaged. Some disease are inherited, others the result of illness or accident, and others are a progression of age.

The most common conditions are:

- **tunnel vision or loss of peripheral vision** (ability to focus on the teacher from two metres away but not the surroundings)

- **loss of central vision** (ability to make out peripheral objects such as trees and the ground but sees only a dark area where the teacher is standing)

- **blurred vision** (when the teacher represents a blurred object)

- **light perception** (sees only light with little or no visual acuity[1])

- **total blindness** (sees only total darkness)

---

1 Visual acuity refers to the clarity or keenness of vision with which a person can see.

Major causes

There are many causes of vision impairment. Whether the vision impairment is congenital or acquired, the major physical result is some form of damage to one or more of the following:

— the eye itself

— the muscles of the eye

— the central nervous system

— the occipital lobe of the brain (the centre for visual identification), and

— the optic nerves which relay information from the eye to the brain.

The most common causes of vision impairment include:

Albinism

Albinism is a congenital hereditary disease resulting in all or some of the body lacking pigment. The most common areas to be affected are the skin, eyes and hair of the person. The severity of pigment loss is unique for each individual. People with pigment loss in their eyes experience severe vision impairment including low visual acuity, nystagmus (jerky movements of the eyes), amblyopia, which affects the transmission of visual information from the eyes to the brain, and photophobia (sensitivity to light). While there is no cure for albinism, glasses and corrective surgery may hinder the development of the disease.

Developmental anomalies

Developmental anomalies can affect the structure of the eye. The most common of these is the cataract. If left untreated (treatment is usually through surgery), a cataract can lead to blindness. Cataracts are the result of a partial or total opacity of the lens and have been likened to looking through a dirty or misty window. Cataracts can occur in any individual.

Defects or diseases

Infections and injuries can result in a number of conditions that affect vision. Some examples are:

• diabetic retinopathy — damage to the retina caused by diabetes mellitus;

• retinoblastoma — a malignant tumour of the eye;

• detached retina — where the inner layers of the retina are separated from the pigment epithelium resulting in focal distortion of visual images, blind spots and/or loss of sight on one side;

• injury from missiles — such as pencils, pens, points of arrows; and

• striking the eye or damage from ultraviolet light from the sun — where visible and invisible light waves cause damage to the retina.

Glaucoma

Glaucoma is one of the most common forms of blindness or vision impairment. It is the result of insufficient drainage from the eyes, causing an increase of intraocular fluid, which in turn increases the pressure in the eye. The optic nerve that takes the visual information to the brain is damaged, and if left untreated this will result in loss of vision. Glaucoma usually affects both eyes, with a gradual, painless loss of vision. Symptoms are commonly unnoticed until severe irreversible damage has occurred. Peripheral vision is the first to be affected.

Refractive errors

These include *myopia* (short-sightedness) where the eyeball is too long from front to back, *hyperopia* (far-sightedness) where the eyeball is too short from front to back, and *astigmatism* caused by defective curvature of the refractive surfaces of the eye resulting in blurred vision.

Retinitis Pigmentosa

A group of inherited diseases, which result in a non-inflammatory progressive degeneration of the retina causing tunnel vision. It first affects the rods responsible for peripheral vision and vision in low light levels, which causes a narrowing of the visual field from the outside, resulting in tunnel vision and poor night vision. As the disease progresses central vision may also be lost. Retinitis Pigmentosa may be accompanied by moderate to severe hearing loss.

Vitamin deficiency

Lack of vitamins may lead to vision impairment and eventual loss. Vitamin A deficiency may lead to night blindness and deterioration of the cornea. Insufficient amounts of vitamin C may cause an ocular haemorrhage. These conditions can be treated with nutritional supplements and are usually reversible if treated early.

Impaired muscle function

Examples of impaired eye muscle function include *nystagmus* (constant involuntary rapid eye movements), *strabismus* (misalignment of the eyes resulting in double vision) and *amblyopia* (referred to as 'lazy eye').

Colour blindness

Occurs where damage to the cones in the retina causes a reduced ability to distinguish between certain colours (usually reds, blues and greens).

Safety concerns

As with any group of people preparing for physical activity, common sense precautions should be taken in order to prevent accidents from happening. This, of course, does not mean that all the 'risk' should be taken out of activity, rather, that reasonable care be taken to ensure a safe environment. While you will need to consider some additional precautions for people with vision impairment do not be overcautious — they too have the right to acquire bumps and bruises.

Implications for physical activity

- Ask the individual what he/she sees — gear your program to their unique needs.

- Discuss general strategies and requirements for the young person with vision impairment with other teachers, parents and/or assistants before beginning a physical activity program.

- Speak clearly and normally: there is no need to raise your voice. Use your normal gestures and use the person's name when addressing him/her. It's OK to use words like 'see' and 'blind' but don't confuse lack of vision with the inability to communicate.

- Introduce yourself when entering a room and let the person know when you are leaving. Describe surroundings as they change and where everyone is sitting so that the individual can direct speech to the appropriate person.

- Do not change the layout of equipment without notifying the individual and take him/her on an orientation walk around the area before activities begin.

- Allow the person with vision impairment to take your arm for guiding — do not grab at or push the individual. Stop when reaching steps or walls so that the individual can prepare for the change — you may have to explain the change that is coming.

- Where possible, and appropriate, provide large print documents for required reading.

- Allow a guide to manually put an individual's hand on the back of a chair when approaching a seat — using the sense of touch is usually enough for the person who is blind to do the rest when it comes to negotiating objects.

- When handing a piece of equipment, such as a ball, to a person who has vision impairment, speak before doing so.

- Do not be afraid to describe to a person with vision impairment the surroundings, such as the weather, what people are wearing, or something funny that happens.

- Remember that oral and tactile stimulation are very important modes of communication for people with vision impairment — incorporate them into your programming.

- Keep in mind the individual's level of residual vision; it will influence the degree of visual demonstration possible.

- Be aware of the age of onset of the individual's condition — if the condition is congenital the rate at which he/she learns various motor skills may differ from his/her sighted peers. While physical fitness and motor skills may be generally inferior there is no evidence to suggest that this is in any way associated with the condition itself. It is more likely to do with lack of opportunity, inappropriate instruction and limited access.

References and further resources

Auxter, D, Pyfer, J and Huettig, C (1993) *Adapted Physical Education and Recreation* (7th ed). St Louis: Mosby-Year Book Inc.

Barker, P and Jones, D, eds (1992) *Disabling World* London: Channel Four Television.

Block, ME (1991) Motor development in children with Down's Syndrome: a review of the literature. *Adapted Physical Activity Quarterly* 8: 179–209.

Block, ME (1994) *A Teacher's Guide to Including Students with Disabilities in Regular Physical Education* Baltimore, Maryland: Paul H Brooks Publishing Co.

Block, ME, Provis, S and Nelson, E (1993) Accommodating students with severe disabilities in regular physical education: extending traditional skill stations *Paleastra* Fall: 32–5.

Bremner, A and Goodman, S (1992) *Coaching Deaf Athletes* Canberra: Australian Sports Commission.

Brissenden, S (1986) Independent living and the medical model. *Disability, Handicap and Society* 1(2).

Cant, H (1990) *Activities Manual for Children with Disabilities* Canberra: Australian Sports Commission.

Connolly, M (1994) Practicum experiences and journal writing in adapted physical education: implications for teacher education. *Adapted Physical Activity Quarterly* 11(3): 206–28.

Davis, K (1986) *Developing Our Own Definitions — Draft for Discussion*. London: British Council of Organisations for Disabled People.

Downs, P (1992) *The attitudes of pre-service physical education students toward the integration of people with disabilities in activity settings — a European comparison* Masters thesis, Loughborough University of Technology, England.

Downs, P (1994) Including students with disabilities in PE. *Aussie Sport Action* 5(4): 7–9.

Downs, P (1995) Strategies for including students with disabilities in regular settings. *Active and Healthy* 2(4): 18–20.

Downs, P (1997) *Project Willing and Able — a Sporting Chance for Young People with Disabilities* Active Connections, 20th Biennial National/International Conference, ACHPER, 80–3.

Downs, P and Prescot, G (1995) Whose right is it anyway? A quick guide to the Disability Discrimination Act. *Aussie Sport Action* 6(2): 35.

Dubowitz, V (1980) *The Floppy Infant* (2nd ed) Clinics in Developmental Medicine, 76. London: Spastics International Publ.

Goodman, S (1993) *Coaching Athletes with Disabilities: General Principles* Canberra: Australian Sports Commission.

Goodman S, Lee, K and Heidt, F (1996) *Coaching Wheelchair Athletes* Canberra: Australian Sports Commission.

Grosse, SJ, Cooper, C, Gavron, S and Stein, J (1989) *The Best of Practical Pointers* Reston, VA: The American Alliance for Health, Physical Education, Recreation and Dance.

Hillary Commission for Sport, Fitness and Leisure (1993) *KiwiAble* Wellington, NZ: Hillary Commission.

Hockey, K and Goodman, S (1992) *Coaching Athletes with Vision Impairments* Canberra: Australian Sports Commission.

Horvat, M (1990) *Physical Education and Sport for Exceptional Students* Dubuque, Iowa: Wm C Brown Publishers.

Humphries, S and Gordon, P (1992) *Out of Sight: the Experience of Disability 1900–1950* Plymouth, England: Northcote House Publishers Ltd.

Jobling, A (1991) *Healthy Lifestyle Issues in Activity Programming for Children with Down's Syndrome* Presentation for the 18th ACHPER National Biennial Conference, Perth.

Jowsey, SE (1992) *Can I Play Too? Physical Education for Physically Disabled Children in Mainstream Schools* London: David Fulton Publishers.

Kennedy, DW, Austin, DR and Smith, RW (1987) *Special Education: Opportunities for Persons with Disabilities* Philadelphia: Saunders College Publishing.

Landrus, RI and Mesibov, GB (1994) *Structured Teaching* North Carolina: University of North Carolina.

Langendorfer, S (1985) Label motor patterns, not kids: a developmental perspective for adapted physical education. *Physical Educator* 42: 175–9.

Lynberg, KL and Danneskiold-Samsoe, B (1988) Exercise training in rheumatoid arthritis. *Scandinavian Journal of Sports Science* 10(2-3): 83–7.

Mahon, MJ (1989) *Physical Education for Students with Special Needs* Manitoba: Manitoba Education and Training.

Meaney, PH, ed. (1993) *Sportstart — Developing Your Kids' Skills at Home* (rev ed), Canberra: Australian Sports Commission.

Morris, J, ed. (1989) *Able Lives: Women's Experience of Paralysis* London: The Women's Press.

Morris, J (1991) *Pride Against Prejudice: Transforming Attitudes to Disability* London: The Women's Press.

Morris, LR and Schulz, L (1989) *Creative Play Activities for Children with Disabilities* (2nd ed) Champaign, Illinois: Human Kinetics Publishers Inc.

Morton, J (1994) *Treating Paediatric Asthma — A Different Approach* Drivetime Radio, Medical Edition 14, Side A-1.

Nunn, CJ (1994) *Coaching Amputee and Les Autres Athletes* Canberra: Australian Sports Commission.

Oliver, M (1992) *The Politics of Disablement* London, Macmillan Press Ltd.

Passentino, E and Cranfield, P (1994) Inclusion at recess: a foundation for friendship. *Palaestra* Fall, 45–8.

Sherrill, C (1993) *Adapted Physical Activity, Recreation and Sport* (4th ed) Dubuque, Iowa: Brown and Benchmark.

Tinning, R, Kirk, D and Evans, J (1993) *Learning to Teach Physical Education* Sydney: Prentice Hall.

Tousignant, M. (1982) *Analysis of Task Structures in Secondary Physical Education Classes* Unpublished Doctoral dissertation, Columbus: Ohio State University.

Winnick, JP (1987) An integration continuum for sport participation. *Adapted Physical Education Quarterly* 4(3): 157–61.

Winnick, JP (1990) *Adapted Physical Education and Sport* Champaign, Illinois: Human Kinetics Publishers Inc.

Wiseman, DC (1994) *Physical Education for Exceptional Students: Theory to Practice* Albany, New York: Delmar Publishers Inc.

Contacts/Help

National and International

Manager — Disability Education Unit
Sport Development Group
Australian Sports Commission
PO Box 176
Belconnen ACT 2616
Tel: (02) 6214 1792
Fax: (02) 6214 1640
email: dep@ausport.gov.au

National Coaching Coordinator —
Disabilities
Australian Sports Commission
PO Box 176
Belconnen ACT 2616
Tel: (02) 6214 1698
Fax: (02) 214 1200
Email: dep@ausport.gov.au

Australian Paralympic Committee
PO Box N570
Grosvenor Place
NSW 1220
Australia

National Sporting Organisations for People with a Disability

AUSRAPID

Suite G4
320 St Kilda Road
Melbourne VIC 3004
Tel: (03) 9696 6206
Fax: (03) 9696 6204

Australian Blind Bowlers Association

4 Isla Street
Sunshine VIC 3020
Tel: (03) 9312 2622

Australian Blind Sport Federation

PO Box 59
Zillmere QLD 4034
Tel: (07) 3865 2043
Fax (07) 3848 4669
Email: absf@ecn.net.au

Australian Blind Cricket Council

8 Valencia Street
Sunnybank QLD 4109
Tel: (07) 3345 2728
Fax: (07) 3848 4669

Australian Deaf Sports Federation Ltd

101–117 Wellington Parade South
East Melbourne VIC 3002
Tel: (03) 9650 2524
Fax: (03) 9654 2868
Web: http://www.deafsports.org.au/

Australian Transplant Sports Association

35 Centre Road
Upwey VIC 3158
Tel: (03) 9754 4736

Australian Sport & Recreation Association for Persons with an Intellectual Disability

Suite G 4
320 St Kilda Road
Melbourne VIC 3004
Tel: (03) 9696 6206
Fax: (03) 9696 6204
Email: ausraned@ozemail.com.au

Australian Sports Organisation for the Disabled Inc

PO Box 3015
Unley SA 5061
Tel: (08) 8410 9233
Fax: (08) 8410 9244

WAPID — Water Activity for People with Integrated Difficulties

PO Box 706
Elizabeth Street SA 5112
Tel: (08) 8254 6033

Cerebral Palsy Australian Sport and Recreation Federation

26 Westaway Street
Sunnybank Hills QLD 4109
Tel: (07) 3345 3775
Fax: (07) 3344 2381
Email: cpasrf@gil.com.au
Web: http://www.cpasrf.gil.com.au/

Disabled Wintersport Australia

15 Beverley Street
Merimbula NSW 2548
Tel: (02) 6495 2082
Fax: (02) 6495 2034
Email: finsko@acr.net.au
Web: http://www.acr.net.au/~skidisabled/

Riding for the Disabled Australia

PO Box 424
Ascot Vale VIC 3023
Tel : (03) 9372 2126
Fax: (03) 9376 6698
Web: http://www.ausport.gov.au/rda/
rdainfo.html

Wheelchair Sports Australia Ltd

John Hogan-Doran
Executive Director
PO Box S83
Homebush South NSW 2140
Tel: (02) 9763 5819
Fax: (02) 9764 3757
Email: awa@ibm.net
Web: http://www.wsa.org.au/

Special Olympics — Australia

PO Box 712
Glebe NSW 2037
Tel: (02) 9552 6188
Fax: (02) 9552 3848

Key State Multidisability Organisations

NSW Sport Council for the Disabled

PO Box 135
Flemington Markets NSW 2129
Tel: (02) 9763 0155
Fax: (02) 9764 374

TAS Sport and Recreation Association for People with a Disability

TASRAD
PO Box 324
Prospect TAS 7250
Tel: (03) 6224 7090
Fax: (03) 6224 3441
Email: tasrad@tassie.net.au

QLD Sporting Wheelies and Disabled

60 Edmonstone Road
Bowen Hills
QUEENSLAND 4006
Tel: (07) 3253 3333
Fax: (07) 3253 3322
Web:
http://www.sportingwheelies.org.au/

WA Disabled Sports Association

PO Box 1162
East Victoria Park WA 6101
Tel: (08) 9470 1442
Fax: (08) 9470 3878

SPARC Disability Foundation State Association House

88 Walkerville Tce
Walkerville SA 5081
Tel: (08) 8342 090
Fax: (08) 8342 0977

VIC Network on Recreation and Disability

179 High Street
Northcote VIC 3070

NT Disabled Sports Association

PO Box 46194
Casuarina NT 0811
Tel: (08) 8948 3069

Appendix 1: Disability Education Program state coordinator contacts

South Australia

Claire Wittwer-Smith
SPARC Disability Foundation
88 Walkerville Terrace
Walkerville SA 5081
Tel: (08) 8342 0900
Fax: (08) 8342 0977
Email: education@sparc.asn.au

Victoria

Kathy Tessier
Active Approach
483 Buckley Street
Essendon VIC 3040
Tel: (03) 9337 0402
Fax: (03) 9337 0408
Mob: 0418 995 986
Email: kathy.tessier@bigpond.com

Queensland

Kelli Chilton
Sporting Wheelies and Disabled Association
60 Edmonstone Road
Bowen Hills QLD 4006
Tel: (07) 3253 3333
Tel: (07) 3253 3322
Email: dep@sportingwheelies.org.au

New South Wales

Lyn Phillips
Sydney Academy of Sport
PO Box 57
Narrabeen NSW 2101
Tel: (02) 9454 0109
Fax: (02) 9454 0133
Email: lphillips@dsr.nsw.gov.au

ACT

Dusty Macgraw
ACT Bureau of Sport and Recreation
PO Box 1156
Tuggeranong ACT 2901
Tel: (02) 6207 2356
Fax: (02) 6207 2071
Email: dusty.macgraw@act.gov.au

Tasmania

Leah Page
TASRAD
PO Box 324
Prospect TAS 7250
Tel: (03) 6336 2012
Fax: (03) 6336 2014
Mob: 0417 362 014
Email: tasrad@tassie.net.au

Western Australia

Richard Lockwood
Dept Human Movement & Exercise Science
University of Western Australia
Nedlands WA 6907
Tel: (08) 9380 2366
Fax: (08) 9380 1039
Email: lockwood@cyllene.uwa.edu.au

Northern Territory

Cathy White
NT Institute of Sport
GPO Box 1141
Casuarina NT 0811
Tel: (08) 8922 6809
Fax: (08) 8922 6800
Email: cathy.white@nt.gov.au

Other DEP contact

Daryl Little (Indigenous Sport Program)
Department of Recreation & Sport
GPO Box 1095
Alice Springs NT 0871
Tel: (08) 8951 6434
Fax: (08) 8951 5330
Email: daryl.little@nt.gov.au

Appendix 2: Lifting techniques

Whilst most people who use wheelchairs will be able to transfer themselves back into their wheelchairs when they have fallen out and be quite capable of moving themselves between chairs, toilets and equipment independently, some may need assistance. As a general rule ask the person if he/she requires assistance and encourage, whenever possible, each individual to perform their own transfers.

The lifting technique described here is the most common, and safest, ground-to-chair lift. One person lifts should be avoided. It is a good idea to brief and practice with a buddy or two before attempting the real thing. Some general lifting guidelines include:

- Lift with the legs and not the back (ie bend the knees before lifting and during lowering rather than bending the lower back).

- It is important for the lifter to keep the centre of gravity of the young person as close to their body as possible to prevent excessive stress on the back

- Lift slowly, smoothly and without jerking.

The two person lift

Position the chair so that it is close to Jane. The upper body lifter should position themselves behind Jane and place their elbows under her arms and clasp their wrists. Instruct Jane to brace her arms and upper body so that a firm lifting base is established. The lifter must then bend their knees so that they are in a straight backed squatting position before the lift begins. The lifter's knees should be split so that one knee is located on each side of Jane's body.

During the lift, in order to distribute the surface area that is receiving the force of the lift as widely as possible, the lifter must use their forearms to grip Jane's chest as well as taking her weight through her bridged arms. The lifter must also hold Jane as close in to their body as possible (ie Jane's back should always be in contact with the lifter's chest).

AUSTRALIAN SPORTS COMMISSION

The lower body lifter should place the arm closest to the chair under Jane's legs. Like the upper body lifter, the lower body lifter must bend their knees so that they are in a straight backed squatting position before the lift begins.

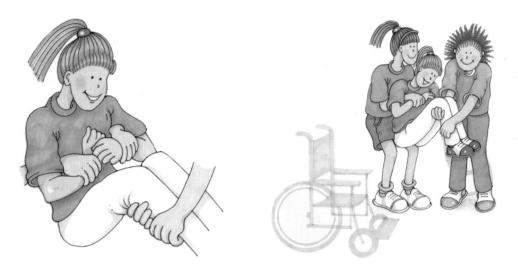

On the count of three, both lifters should firmly and simultaneously lift Jane with their legs until they are both in an upright position.

Once both lifters are upright, they should then shuffle across to a position where Jane is above her chair. The lifters should then gradually lower Jane into her chair, ensuring that as they do so they bend their knees rather than their backs.

Appendix 3: Schools Network membership form

ACTIVE AUSTRALIA

Schools Network

Registration form

Complete the registration form and fax to:

National Coordinator Active Australia Schools

ACHPER, 214 Port Road, Hindmarsh SA 5007 Tel (08) 8340 3388 Fax (08) 8340 3399

Name of contact person ....

Name of school ....

Address for mailing ....

....

.... Postcode ....

Telephone .... Facsimile ....

Email ....

School type: ☐ Government   ☐ Catholic   ☐ Independent

☐ Primary   ☐ Secondary   ☐ Other

Reason for interest ....

....

....

....

Appendix 4: School environment/ethos form

Objective: Our school will provide a supportive environment for all members of the school and the local community to be physically active.

Our strengths/Achievements	

Areas for improvement	Actions

Appendix 5: Graph depicting assistance/independence

At the end of an activity or lesson in which you have assisted a student with a disability, take a moment to plot the level of their dependence/independence. To do this, simply locate the percentage (vertical axis) of the task in which you were directly involved in instruction, demonstration, or completion, and match it to the corresponding percentage (horizontal axis) which indicates the student's active involvement.

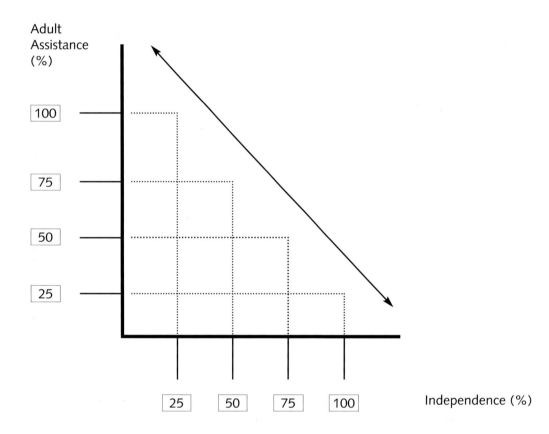

In many areas of academic functioning, students with disabilities are reliant on others (most often teacher aides rather than teachers) to assist them in completing tasks in the classroom setting. Often this guidance does not follow the same procedure as instruction to a student without disabilities. Therefore, on many occasions the student is guided, both in their thinking and performance, by an adult, employing adult reasoning, influenced and shaped by years of experience.

In such instances the student is required to passively accept previously unencountered concepts, and indeed whole chunks of information as being correct, without having first-hand experience. The result is that we think the student understands the concept or has the skill, when the activity has been successfully completed. The question is, *how much of the activity was guided or even completed by the adult, and how much was done by the student?*

Appendix 6: School community links form

Objective: Our school will promote and provide for physical activity in collaboration with the local community.

Our Strengths/Achievements	
Areas for improvement	**Actions**

Appendix 7: Curriculum teaching and learning policy form

Objective: Our school will develop and implement policies and curriculum practices that reflect the importance and benefits of physical activity.

Our Strengths/Achievements

Areas for improvement	Actions

Appendix 8: Client focus checklist

Client focus	1	2	3	4	5	Evidence/action	Date achieved
1. We know who our clients are							
2. We gather information about our clients' needs and expectations							
3. We design our activities, products and services to satisfy those needs and expectations without sacrificing financial viability							
4. We regularly review our performance in meeting client needs and expectations							

1 Have not considered   2 Thinking about it   3 Starting to develop   4 Implementing   5 Achieving and monitoring

Appendix 9: Human resources checklist

Human resources	1	2	3	4	5	Evidence/action	Date achieved
1. There is a friendly and welcoming atmosphere in our club or organisation							
2. We plan our people needs, including what skills and/or qualifications we require and what training may be needed							
3. We have policies and practices that encourage access and equity							
4. We have enough people with skills or qualifications to carry out all necessary tasks							

1 Have not considered   2 Thinking about it   3 Starting to develop   4 Implementing   5 Achieving and monitoring

AUSTRALIAN SPORTS COMMISSION

Appendix 10: Audit sheet

Accessibility	Yes/no	Brainstorm solutions
• Location *How can new members access your club?* *Is the club close to transport?*		
• Parking/drop offs *Do members or drivers need accessible parking? Are the car parks close to entrances? Is the surface of the car park suitable for people with mobility difficulties? Is there a procedure to ensure that people are safe on arrival or departure?*		
• Welcome procedure *Tour of facility* *How are members welcomed? How are they supported in their introduction to the club? Is there a check to ensure that they have settled in?*		
• Signage *Do signs indicate important features (eg reception, toilets, canteen, exit)? Are they clearly written and visible? Are universal symbols used?*		
• Ramps/pathways *Is there a clear, safe pathway joining all main features? Are all areas easily accessed by people with mobility difficulties?*		

Appendix 10: Audit sheet (continued)

Accessibility	Yes/no	Brainstorm solutions
• Toilets *Are toilets located for quick access?* *Are they suitable for mobility difficulties?* *Is privacy assured for all people?*		
• Activity environments *Is the facility safe and clear of clutter?* *Can people move about independently?* *Is the area adequately lit, cooled* *and heated?*		
• Resources (human, physical and financial) *Does the club have the necessary* *equipment to support inclusion?* *Are additional support staff required?* Policies and procedures *Are there provisions for addressing people* *with disabilities? Is there a grievance* *procedure to address issues? Is there a* *procedure to ensure activity staff are aware* *of medical issues?* Training and information *Do coaches or other staff need additional* *training? Do other members of the club* *need additional training? Are members,* *coaches and other staff supportive of* *people with disabilities?*		

AUSTRALIAN SPORTS COMMISSION

Appendix 11: Quality of service checklist

Quality of service	1	2	3	4	5	Evidence/action	Date achieved
1. Our aims and practices are directed toward satisfying our clients with disabilities							
2. We have appropriate procedures for our activities to ensure they are always carried out well							
3. We continually review all aspects of our standard of service for the purpose of planning and improvement							
4. We involve all appropriate stakeholders in our reviews							

1 Have not considered   2 Thinking about it   3 Starting to develop   4 Implementing   5 Achieving and monitoring